Family Learning in the Early Years

Using theory and practice to explore partnerships between professionals and families, *Family Learning to Inclusion in the Early Years* adds to current expertise through deeper insight into the complexities of inclusion within a specific context of family learning. The book presents inclusive practice which reflects the individuality of each child. Application of a therapeutic approach to promote, or to minimise, behaviour through self-regulation is demonstrated to the reader by illustrative examples. Hazel G. Whitters emphasises the value of supporting every child at the very beginning of a lifelong learning journey by activating the vocational skills of the early years' workforce.

Beginning with a discussion of the concept of family in the 21st century, descriptive scenarios help readers to link theory to the reality of daily practice in a clear and useful way. The book presents a generational cycle of development through a theoretical and practical perspective, and explains how practice can contribute to closing the implementation gap within a context of family learning and inclusion in the early years. It encourages exchange of knowledge and understanding on issues, prompting readers' reflection, re-configuration, discussion, dissent, argument, or agreement.

An essential read for any in the field of inclusive lifelong learning, this book will be of interest to academics, post-graduate students, and researchers in the field of early years' education, as well as those working within services.

Hazel G. Whitters is a senior early years' worker and child protection officer in a voluntary organisation in Glasgow, Scotland. She has conducted research in child protection and early intervention.

Family Learning to Inclusion in the Early Years
Theory, Practice, and Partnerships

Hazel G. Whitters

LONDON AND NEW YORK

First published 2018 by Routledge

2 Park Square, Milton Park, Abingdon, Oxon OX14 4RN
605 Third Avenue, New York, NY 10017

Routledge is an imprint of the Taylor & Francis Group, an informa business

First issued in paperback 2021

Copyright © 2018 Hazel G. Whitters

The right of Hazel G. Whitters to be identified as author of this work has been asserted by her in accordance with sections 77 and 78 of the Copyright, Designs and Patents Act 1988.

All rights reserved. No part of this book may be reprinted or reproduced or utilised in any form or by any electronic, mechanical, or other means, now known or hereafter invented, including photocopying and recording, or in any information storage or retrieval system, without permission in writing from the publishers.

Notice:
Product or corporate names may be trademarks or registered trademarks, and are used only for identification and explanation without intent to infringe.

Publisher's Note

The publisher has gone to great lengths to ensure the quality of this reprint but points out that some imperfections in the original copies may be apparent.

British Library Cataloguing-in-Publication Data
A catalogue record for this book is available from the British Library

Library of Congress Cataloging-in-Publication Data
A catalog record for this book has been requested

ISBN: 978-1-138-47908-1 (hbk)
ISBN: 978-0-367-37147-0 (pbk)

Typeset in Times New Roman
by Apex CoVantage, LLC

I dedicate this book to my own family – mum and dad, sisters Margaret and Fiona, and especially to my husband John.

Your wisdom, support, and encouragement have enabled me to learn, and to share my understanding with others.

Thank you!

Contents

	Introduction	viii
1	Families and the earliest years	1
2	Special needs to inclusion	29
3	Leading the workforce: practice to policy	61
	Index	74

Introduction

Family Learning to Inclusion in the Early Years: Theory, Practice, and Partnerships prioritises the influence from primary carers upon a child's development within the context of early years' services. The content promotes pedagogy which supports inclusion by accessing the expertise of a child's parents and extended family.

Family learning is a multi-faceted concept which is activated within the early years' sector through partnership-working between professionals, parents, and families. This book promotes the necessity to review and revise implementation based upon historical beliefs, and to focus upon pedagogy which reflects the most up-to-date knowledge and understanding. Current and past policy are considered, as well as the development of inclusive pedagogy which incorporates influences from each child's world. This book is not attempting to replicate knowledge which has been promoted by previous authors, but it seeks to add to current expertise through deeper insight into the complex concept of inclusion, in a specific context of family learning.

Family may encompass a birth mother, birth father, step-mother or step-father, same-sex partners, formal or informal kinship care, foster-carer, adoptive parent, or a combination of these sources of attachment figures. The term *parent* will be used throughout this book to represent the primary carer of a child.

Comprehension of learning has developed from formal teaching by an educator to practice relating to "scaffolding", "sustained-shared thinking", reciprocity, inter-subjectivity, and secure attachment between a child and his or her primary and secondary carers. Teaching and learning are interdependent features throughout our lifespans, and the context of early years' settings provides rich developmental opportunities for child and parent. The therapeutic approach underpins current practice and recognises families as essential collaborators in supporting our youngest citizens to learn and to achieve potential.

Implementation of the early years' curriculum has evolved from adult-led structured lessons to child-centred practice, and ultimately to child-led active learning in the 21st century. This movement in early years reflects changes in society and policy which have given recognition to a child's individual rights, in addition to the rights of a child within a family unit. The learning environment in childhood has developed from informal parent and toddler groups, to formal regulated organisations, and finally to family services. The family services use principles of best practice which recognise the complementariness of skill and expertise of the primary parental carer, and professional.

Research in neuroscience and longitudinal studies have transformed understanding of the impact of care and education, before the birth until the age of five, to involvement and wellbeing throughout childhood and adulthood. A therapeutic, pedagogical approach which recognises the role of a family can complement the use of interventions and resources. The early years' curriculum can be underpinned through implementation beyond the organisational environment, for example, within the family home.

I encounter services in a state of flux due to influences from old and new approaches. Sustainability is essential for every organisation, and good practice evolves over many years of service delivery. This book explores the concepts of organisational memory and intellectual curiosity in the early years' workplace, and considers the importance of pedagogy in maintaining best practice approaches despite changes in personnel.

The processes associated with *optimising learning for all children* have led to practitioners having an increase in comprehension of human development, and the impact of internal and external factors upon each child and parent. Minute aspects of learning and development are explored by using theory and examples of practice in the field. The concept of resilience is also investigated and discussed in a context of professional support for children who face adversities from trauma or learning needs. The book aims to support the early years' workforce in accessing transferrable skills, and realising professional potential in this current aspect of practice.

The inclusion debate has rapidly added complexity to these issues over the past two decades. The concept of inclusion, in which all children attend mainstream services, is topical, potentially controversial, and causing early years' practitioners to review their professional skills, ability, and capacity to support optimum outcomes for every child in their care. Teaching, caring, and nurturing continue to be integral features of the early years' role, and inclusive pedagogy has been enhanced by embracing family members as co-constructors in a child's educational journey. The implementation gap is reviewed in this context from a strategic and operational perspective. Firstly, the importance of transferring recommendations from research to policy and guidance, and using theory to enrich daily practice. Secondly, recognising the value of practice as an influence upon policy development. I have become aware of gaps in the comprehension of early years' professionals regarding inclusion. After a presentation, I am often approached by attendees (usually senior staff or post-graduate researchers) who are seeking out specific strategies on three aspects of current early years' work:

- How to react to challenging behaviours and manage a mainstream setting
- How to support learning for each child within a mixed-ability group
- How to give emotional support and raise the morale of the professional team

These examples indicate that adult-led pedagogy is being sought so that children conform to the traditional mainstream setting. I feel that this presents an area in which an impact could be made upon the implementation gap from the point of practice: operational to strategic.

I am passionate about supporting the early years' workforce and parents to gain ability and capacity to comprehend the child's perspective. This realisation will empower primary and secondary carers to identify and apply innovative approaches which are child led, and adhere to inclusive pedagogy. Inclusion in practice is dependent upon a partnership of a professional and parent collaborating together to assess, understand, and respond to the needs of each child. A significant aspect is observing and interpreting the child's communicative strategies in the form of behaviour, and reaction to learning environments in the home and within services. The pressure of managing a classroom, nursery playroom, or home environment is alleviated if children can become active participants in learning and regulating their behaviour.

This book is not about generic strategies, but about activating the vocational skills of the early years' workforce through an increase in understanding, and promoting the value of supporting every child at the very beginning of a lifelong learning journey.

Chapter 1, "Families and the earliest years", introduces the topic by discussing the concept of family in the 21st century. *Fractured, broken, split, single parent, unmarried mother,* and *absent father* are historical descriptive terms which imposed disadvantage upon a family through implication of sub-standard parenting. Current understanding of *family* is associated with the ability and capacity to care, educate, and nurture a child by one or more attachment figures. Environments and learning in the early years are reviewed from parent and toddler groups to registered nurseries and family services. Illustrative examples give clarity to the reader in linking theoretical frameworks to the minutiae of daily practice which is informed by professionals and parents working together. Two theories are presented to support comprehension of the topic by focusing upon the professional–parent relationship, and the process of learning.

Chapter 2, "Special needs to inclusion", focuses upon the professional–parent partnerships within the context of inclusion in the early years. A generational cycle of development is presented through a theoretical and practical perspective of family learning. This chapter explores inclusion within pedagogy which recognises the individuality of each child. Needs are often identified in relation to a child's *age*, and expectations of development. Chapter 2 discusses need from each child's perspective in accordance with his or her *stage* of development. Support mechanisms for practitioners are identified, and they include the expertise of primary carers within a family. The understanding and application of a therapeutic approach to promote learning and social behaviour is demonstrated to the reader through practice examples from the early years' setting. Additionally, the change of focus from adult management of a child's behaviour to self-regulation and resilience to adversity is linked to inclusive pedagogy, and capacity for learning and achieving throughout a lifespan.

Chapter 3, "Leading the workforce: practice to policy", explains how practice can contribute to closing the implementation gap within a context of family learning and inclusion in the early years. A potential dichotomy is highlighted between the recording of statistics relative to curricular outcomes, and recognition of each child's executive functioning and achievement of potential. The concepts of organisational memory and intellectual curiosity are discussed and associated with sustainability of good practice. This chapter concludes with key messages.

1 Families and the earliest years

Family

Comprehension of the concept of family has changed over the past 20 years: *fractured, broken, split, single parent, unmarried mother,* and *absent father* are historical descriptive terms which imposed disadvantage upon a family through implication of sub-standard parenting. Current understanding of *family* is associated with the ability and capacity to provide care, to educate, and to nurture a child by one or more attachment figures.

No longer is a family depicted as mother, father, and 2.4 children. Family in today's society is regarded as the primary carers for children in childhood and adolescence, and potentially influential throughout the lifespan. Family may encompass a birth mother, birth father, step-mother or step-father, same-sex partners, formal or informal kinship care from a relative, foster-carer, adoptive parent, or a combination of these sources of attachment figures. The term of *parent* will be used throughout this book to represent the primary carer of a child. Bowlby (1979) promoted a secure attachment to a responsive adult as essential to a child's wellbeing and to development. The ability and capacity to respond effectively to a child's emotional, intellectual, and physical needs, and interests are key attributes to the role of primary carer in the context of a *family*, and secondary carer in the context of a *professional*. Research indicates that parents create a link between professional role and concepts associated with family (Whitters, 2009).

Formal family learning: legislation

The link between parents' involvement and a child's education was recognised formally in Scotland in 2006 through publication of the Parental Involvement Act (Scottish Government, 2006). This legislation referred to learning within schools, and it promoted parents as primary educators, integral to raising attainment. The 2006 Act identified three environments in which parents could potentially contribute to education within a framework. Emphasis was given to *parents* initiating involvement through the following links:

1 Learning at home
2 Home/school partnerships
3 Parental representation for example on parent–school boards

A review of this legislation 10 years later identified six ways in which parents could become involved in shaping and supporting their child's education (The National Parent Forum of Scotland, 2017). It is interesting to note that a decade after the first parenting act, the onus on parental participation was linked to the *professional bodies*, in this case, schools.

1 Positive parenting: families should be supported by the school to create positive parenting environments in the home.
2 Services should communicate effectively with parents and promote relevant information regarding school programmes.
3 Services should facilitate the inclusion of volunteers to support children.
4 Services should create home–school links.
5 Services should seek out and action the opinions of parents in school decision-making.
6 Services should integrate families with local community provision.

Findings from this review identified that professionals and parents had an increased awareness of the importance of liaising together regarding children's education and attainment. Data showed that this legislation did not encompass education in the early years of childhood, but a recommendation to address this issue has been forwarded to Scottish Government (2017b) at the time of publication.

The United Kingdom Nurture Network reviewed the nurturing approach in schools which responded to children's social, emotional, and behavioural issues (Nurture Network, 2017). The authors identified that principles should be applied by pupils, education staff, *and* parents to achieve the most effective nurturing approach within this context of education.

Adversities associated with parental skills dominate the list of "common stressors" for children as depicted in this review; however, the assessment tool, in the form of Boxall Profile, is described and promoted as supporting *teachers* to understand and to respond to social and emotional difficulties of children in their care. It may be that teachers share their increase in knowledge and subsequent understanding with parents, but this aspect is not presented in the publication. It is important that these issues are clearly communicated at every available opportunity to reduce the implementation gap from research to practice: promoting academic and practice links.

Culture of family and community learning

The ethos of *creating a culture of family and community learning* was applied in Scotland within the Early Years' Framework in 2008, and reference was made to the use of parenting programmes (Scottish Government, 2008b). This Framework represented a fresh approach as a concordat between Scottish Government and council of Scottish local authorities (COSLA) which focused upon early years and early intervention. The Framework identified 10 key elements for progress which had been informed by evidence collated through inspectorate. The data were used to assess and to evaluate potential links between parenting programmes, raising attainment in a curricular context, and identification of additional achievement. The focus, at this stage of guidance and legislation, was to support a child's engagement with education by encouraging involvement in parenting programmes.

Additionally, the workforce skills, qualifications, and attitude are highlighted as integral to implementation of early intervention in the framework context. Attainment of children was representative of a positive outcome, and secondary output related to empowerment of families and communities. A future aim was to re-focus upon building the capacity of individuals through service provision as opposed to positive outcomes relating to specific interventions.

This is the first Scottish document which promotes *professional attitude* within the 10 elements of transformational change for a nation. The roles of voluntary and private sector early years' services also feature within the 10 elements, and they are linked to *innovative and holistic implementation*. The term *partnership* is used in this context to indicate the necessity for collaboration between universal – health, education, and social work, and targeted services – voluntary and private sectors.

Professional–parent relationship – the therapeutic alliance

Knowledge of the professional–parent relationship, sometimes termed *the therapeutic alliance* (Rogers, 1990), has transformed the delivery of early years' services throughout the world within a context of family learning (Cara and Brooks, 2012; Dalli, 2014; Scottish Government, 2016). The development of relational skills has been recognised as an essential component of practice (Department for Children, Schools and Families, 2009; Scottish Government, 2008a).

Research into the effect of multiple carers on children's developmental progress identified a positive outcome of the professional–parent relationship as consistency in responses to children's need by primary and secondary carers (Siraj-Blatchford, Sylva, Muttock, Gilden and Bell, 2002). The relationship is a medium which represents a mesosystem by creating links between two microsystems in the child's daily life: the home environment and early years' service.

The study was called The Effective Provision of Pre-School Education Project (Department for Education and Skills, 2004). Findings were widely disseminated throughout early years' services in the United Kingdom, and recommendations continue to be used to inform guidance materials for practitioners. The relationship has the potential to support transference of informational, instrumental, and emotional support from educator to developing person, the parent. This inter-personal human connection also has the potential to support transference of knowledge and understanding of the child from parent, as primary carer, to the professional, as the secondary carer.

Joseph (2015) emphasises the significance of this relationship as promoting value and acceptance to the parent. The effect of a therapeutic alliance is to encourage development of self-determination in a parent to support a process of change, and to activate the inner resources. Each person stores knowledge and understanding from every experience which influences the formation of perceptions, and interpretation of the world. Bowlby (1979) used the term *inner working model*. The use of this reference framework in executive functioning, and basic reactions to proximal and distal environments, indicates that the attitude and belief of an early years' worker are significant attributes which influence actions, behaviour and emotions of the service-provider and service-user. Role-modelling by the professional, within the context of a relationship, is a potent source of learning for the parent, in addition to descriptive praise, and affirmation of progress.

Her Majesty's (HM) Government also recognised the significance of working with families in the Early Years' Foundation Stage of 2008, which was subsequently updated in 2012 (HM Government, 2008a, 2012). Parental involvement features in the Children and Families Act 2014 through association with child welfare (HM Government, 2014), and the Children and Young Peoples (Scotland) Act 2014 (Scottish Government, 2014). Insertion of aims and strategies into legislation can add to the impact factor of any concept upon practice and raise awareness which may increase the potential for funding opportunities to be sourced or directly offered by funders. In addition, legislation can impose accountability which is a factor in maintaining consistent good practice by individuals, organisations, local authorities, and throughout a country.

HM Government acknowledged the importance of consistent implementation of the Foundation Stage by presenting the workforce with a practice tool to evaluate and to respond to the needs of each child in a context of *every child matters* – the Common Assessment Framework for Children and Young People (HM Government, 2008b). Also, recognition was given to upskilling early years' practitioners to practice effectively in six identified areas of expertise (HM Government, 2008c):

- Effective communication and engagement
- Child and young person development
- Safeguarding and promoting the welfare of children
- Supporting transitions
- Multi-agency working
- Sharing information

The purpose of this publication was continuous professional development for practitioners in the field, and an opportunity was taken to promote the role and responsibilities of parents as integral to learning for the next generation. I have often observed a change in power within the professional–parent dyad following professional development, whether in the form of qualifications or in-service training. Service-providers may adopt a perspective of *parenting expert* either openly or subliminally. Research has indicated that a professional stance as parenting expert can cause tension in partnerships with primary carers which is based upon professionals merging their responsibilities and their expectations of parents (Van Houte, Bradt, Vandenbroeck, and Bouverne-De Bie, 2013). It is useful that guidance documentation reminds employees that parents should be respected as the primary educators of their children.

Implementation of family learning

Harris and Goodall (2007) linked parental engagement, defined as supporting learning in the home environment, to socio-economic status of the family and parents' historical experience of education. The descriptor of "hard to reach" is used to represent families who operate in a context of adversities which may minimise engagement with services. This research promoted an important message to practitioners by emphasising processes associated with implementation of interventions.

Implementation can refer to the delivery by a service-provider of a parenting programme, and the participation processes of service-users, as parents. A review of international programmes identified *cultural sensitivity* as a facilitatory feature during implementation (Moran, Ghate, and van der Merwe, 2004). Cultural sensitivity generally refers to practitioner's responses to the needs, circumstances, perceptions, and beliefs of the parent and child. Moran et al. described three different approaches which were based on their research data:

1 **Translation** – the parenting programme is translated into the home language of the participants. This approach could increase engagement and motivation of participants, but it may result in misinterpretation of ideas, actions, and context. An interpreter who is not trained to deliver the programme may not relay information to participants with the same intent or understanding as the facilitator.
2 **Culturally adapted** – the original values and principles in the parenting programme are adapted to take into account local cultural beliefs. These beliefs could relate to race, religion, sexuality, lifestyles, or range of other factors which affect daily living for participant group. This approach could create a strong link between knowledge acquisition, comprehension, and an increase in practical parenting skills. It may also result in the integrity of the programme being questioned, and could affect consistency of implementation between countries or local areas, and evaluation of data collection for research purposes.
3 **Culturally specific** – a parenting programme which responds to a local culture is created. Culture can encompass race, religion, belief, circumstances/lifestyle, and additional support for learning needs. This approach creates challenges in the creation of a culturally specific programme which is based upon research evidence, adheres to the demands of funders, and can be sanctioned by a local authority or government.

Perceptions of family learning

The term *family learning* was applied in legislation launched in Scotland in 2012 in the form of the National Parenting Strategy. The Strategy actions this national aspiration by recognising the skillsets of parents (Scottish Government, 2012). The document promoted the significant role of parents as primary educators to their children, in addition to having a key role in shaping society. The publication outlined financial commitment to services from the government to support the delivery of parenting intervention over a range of issues which encompassed health, education, and wellbeing. Comprehension and expectations associated with the parental role in education had developed alongside concepts linked to involvement, engagement, and partnership. Understanding of education had also been extended to include the earliest years of childhood.

This Scottish document does use descriptors which are reminiscent of the historical terms identified in the opening of this chapter, but these terms are applied to acknowledge specific needs in order to create a direct link to targeted funding. Examples are parents of disabled children, parents of teenagers, families affected by imprisonment, families affected by domestic abuse, families of looked-after children – birth parents, foster and kinship carers, and adoptive parents. These descriptions emphasise the circumstances of each family as opposed to implication of poor parenting; however, the document also refers to parental status in the form of lone parents, single fathers, and teenage parents. Terms which are used in published documents are open to misinterpretation by politicians, professionals, parents, and general public. The result may lead to stereotypical assumptions about individuals if the parenting ability is linked to perceived negative circumstances of the family, in opposition to traditional nuclear families who are tacitly associated with positive parenting.

Evaluation of family learning

Research by HM Government in 2012 highlighted a lack of evidence regarding the wider benefits of family learning for parents (Cara and Brooks, 2012); however, the findings did identify an increase in parents' skills which related to social capital. Lee (2008) referred to social capital as family relationships which support development of a child, but this term is often broadened to encompass benefit to a community and indeed a nation.

The Scottish Government conducted a review of family learning in 2016 which had a national and international research database (Scottish Government, 2016). An additional outcome of family learning had been identified since publication of the Early Years' Framework in 2008. In 2016, family learning is described as contributing to *equity in society,* and this term features in the title of the publication. Titles of publications have great significance in electronic searches for information, and subsequently breadth of dissemination. It is often the case that a title promotes a summary of content, rationale, or expected outcome.

Recent research indicated that countries should increase the emphasis on family learning within the earliest years of childhood to impact upon disadvantage and poverty in society (National Institute of Adult Continuing Education, 2013; Save the Children, 2013). Results showed that the use of family learning, as an approach to early intervention, could increase the level of children's development by 15 per cent in a context of disadvantaged groups. Findings also highlighted and placed significance upon the longitudinal effect of family learning beyond the parameters of a specific programme.

Family learning as applied in practice throughout the United Kingdom refers to the processes of learning in addition to potential and expected outcomes. Expectations of outcomes are usually promoted by funders in the context of parenting programmes, and based upon evidence within the research which informed adoption of a specific programme. Heckman (2011) stated that investing in policy, in a context of early years, promotes equity and economic efficiency for a country by impacting upon inequalities in society at an opportune period. This researcher made an interesting point in saying that high-quality parenting can exist alongside adversity linked to poverty, but *high income does not* necessarily guarantee positive parenting.

An evaluation of family learning was also commissioned in 2017 by the Department for Education (Boxford et al., 2017). The aim was to evaluate an intervention targeted specifically for families of adolescents termed The Family Learning Intervention Programme. Initial findings recommend that the theory of change, upon which the programme is constructed, should be refined in order to place greater emphasis upon strengthening family relationships. Family relationships are sustainability factors for change, particularly in a context of child protection.

Informal family learning

Parents have always sought out peer support for their children through community links in the proximal environment, for example interactions with neighbours, and distal environment in the form of leisure and educational facilities. Parents will often seek out collegiate support in this context and absorb the local culture through integration with other families. Community groups emphasise that a parent is the child's prime educator. The names of parenting support groups have changed over the last 20 years. Current terms reflect the significance which society gives to input from any parental carer regardless of gender or age. For example, Mother and Toddler Groups have been re-named Parent and Toddler or Carer and Toddler Groups. In the United Kingdom, there are some groups specifically for fathers, but generally these informal social gatherings welcome any child, and any adult who represents the parenting role. Emphasis has also been given to promoting the content, and potential output from these community groups, for example:

- Care and Share
- Stay and Play
- Play and Learn
- Bounce and Rhyme
- Book-Bug: parents and children
- Tots Gym: health and wellbeing
- Tots Dancing: fitness and fun

This approach to advertising a service presents clear choices to parents which can empower primary carers to consider their children's needs and to gain comprehension of developmental opportunities out-with the family. It also reflects an increase in knowledge, of service-provider and service-user, regarding a range of environments which impact upon a child's learning in the earliest years. Anecdotal evidence indicates that parents attend drop-in groups which adhere to the parents' own interests or ambitions for their children covering topics such as dancing, literacy, and singing.

Social media

Social media has a significant role in disseminating information between primary carers locally or throughout the world. This form of communication has to some extent replaced direct verbal interaction between neighbours in a community, and peer support for parents is often based upon a common issue. For example, in Glasgow, the Chinese community have a vibrant Facebook page in Mandarin and Cantonese, which is an invaluable parent-led resource to support integration into local communities and beyond.

Example from practice

One wet June morning, a young Chinese mother, Sii Fang, came into the family centre with a friend. Sii Fang had been attending the service with her two little boys for a year. This family arrived in London one year ago, seeking asylum. Following several "homeless moves", Sii Fang, her husband Feng, and the two boys were accommodated in an inner-city area of Scotland and joined our service.

Sii Fang introduced me to Xie Xie and her twin girls who were sitting side by side in a double buggy, smiling despite the raindrops which I noticed had made their straight black fringes shine. Xie Xie had been in the area for one month and made contact with the Chinese community through Facebook. My challenge was completing a council six page application form with Xie Xie for her two little girls to access nursery places. This Mandarin-speaking mother competently produced her communication device – a mobile phone – and she rapidly selected a Mandarin-English app! Sii Fang and I exchanged glances – I pointed to her friend Xie Xie, gave a broad smile and universal thumbs up – Xie Xie giggled and spoke a few Mandarin words in excitement as our therapeutic relationship commenced . . .   .

This significant moment transcends potential barriers as Chinese parent, and Scottish practitioner, bow their heads together to study Mandarin-English text on a mobile phone, which results in the use of our worldwide language of laughter and shared understanding.

Electronic devices represent media which have transformed communication between service-users and service-providers who have different home languages. I have also encountered a recent use of mobile phone apps by parents, who have additional support for learning needs, in communicating information on a particular issue, often relating to health, finances, or potential educational needs of a child. The use of e-communication can contribute to creation of a therapeutic alliance if it is used to add clarity to information sharing and to facilitate direct interaction between a professional and parent, in person.

- The e-medium is easily transferrable between different learning environments.
- It is commonly used and understood by professionals and parents.
- It can be used by service-provider or service-user.
- It has a quick response time.

No longer is communication between cultures based solely upon exchange of factual information. No longer does a vulnerable parent have to remain in a service-foyer, unsure, and potentially afraid, as a professional waits in a phone queue to access an interpreter's helpdesk. No longer does communication exclusively rely upon the use of a third party which can impose an unpredictable, external influence upon the professional–parent partnership.

Electronic information exchange is increasingly used by parents to access advice on a specific parenting issue or to gain a range of skills. There are numerous websites available which promote general information or advice which is relevant to an identified need. Help-seeking is a sign of active parenting, and families are keen to carry out their roles and responsibilities from an informed base of knowledge and understanding. Many families are scattered throughout the world due to economic or social issues, and accessing support from extended family members is not always achievable.

Research has identified positive and potentially negative outcomes from this rapid development in communication technology and the application in a context of parenting. Parents may become agents of change; however child protection issues can be hidden from services (Lamberton, Devaney, and Bunting, 2016). This electronic approach to learning can support primary carers to become active participants in the development of their skills, therefore directly responding to parental responsibility and accountability. Online technology used in the privacy of a home environment or mobile device is perceived as granting anonymity by the primary carer. An easily accessible route to queries is attractive and popular with this generation of parents, but precludes interpretation of circumstances as applicable to each family, and it only promotes generic informational support.

Accessing electronic information is a direct signalling of need by a parent, and the response is dependent on the search descriptors within the request. The parent, from a perspective of learner, subsequently actions the information in the form of parenting behaviour towards a child. The actions cannot be supported by emotional and social guidance relative to the personal context. Child protection issues may be difficult for services to identify from online contact with parents. If potential concerns are highlighted, then the electronic medium may create a barrier to clarification, or delay responsive action by services. Also, parents may not be aware that their inquiries could be interpreted in a context of child protection. Electronic-based parenting support in the United Kingdom today presents many challenges to practitioners in understanding the needs of *parents and children* as described online, and using personalised responding.

What does this mean in theory and practice?

- Direct signalling of need is the first step to being an agent of change.
- The electronic medium used is concurrent with the base of knowledge and available tools of the 21st century.
- The power of involvement is retained by the service-user – parent.
- The power of knowledge is held by the service-provider – professional – but shared with the developing parent.
- Parenting advice in response to an electronic query is limited to using information sourced within the microsystem, as portrayed by a parent, and excludes use of a therapeutic relationship.

Urie Bronfenbrenner presented a theoretical framework to support comprehension of human development which has been greatly influential to research and practice (Bronfenbrenner, 1979). The simplistic format of four concentric circles belies the complexity of concepts which underpin this theory. Four sources of influential factors to learning were identified, and termed *systems*. Each system was granted a prefix by Bronfenbrenner to qualify the meaning. Each prefix represented the position of the source, or the purpose in relation to the human being; however, the proximity to a developing person did not equate with an impact value upon development.

1   The *microsystem* represents influences nearest to the person, within the proximal environment of daily life which may affect perceptions and attitude.
2   The *mesosystem(s)*, in an intermediary role, supports transitional impact of influences by creating uni-directional and bi-directional links between microsystems.

3 The *exosystem* contains influences which have an indirect impact on the individual.
4 The *macrosystem* is the source of indirect influences within the distal environment which affect knowledge and understanding.

Latterly Bronfenbrenner (2005) acknowledged an additional effect from human biology, and subsequently re-named the theory as the Bio-Ecological Systems Theory of Human Development.

Bronfenbrenner (1979) identified direct peer influences as located in the microsystem. Parenting styles, which are demonstrated by parents in the earliest stages after birth, reflect personal experience of childcare in addition to influences from social and cultural environments. The extensive use of social media within current communication networks has widened the availability of influences which impact directly or indirectly upon parenting knowledge, understanding, perceptions, attitude, and ultimately style of interaction with a child. Parents can easily access legislation, guidance, and research from around the world via websites on a mobile phone. This use of information technology potentially changes understanding of the positioning of influences within the theoretical framework. For example, if a parent accesses information from a government website on eligibility for childcare support then this influence could be regarded as originating within the macrosystem; however the use of a mobile phone can appear to personalise the exchange of factual information, and potentially influence perceptions and attitude within a microsystem. This is an area of family learning for future research.

Harvard research team use the term *complementary learning* in reference to family support from a range of sources (Harvard Family Research Project, 2006), and in the 21st century, this range could be extended across the microsystem, mesosystem, exosystem, and macrosystem due to the impact from versatile and innovative methods of communication.

Supporting active family learning

Family learning may take place in the presentation of learning activities within the family home, for example, the Baby Box project which was launched throughout Scotland (Scottish Government, 2017a). Every new parent receives a delivery of basic equipment and toys, and the pilot research indicated that this informal intervention will contribute to reducing inequalities related to poverty, in addition to informing parental responses to sleeping routines, development of attachment, and support parent–child interactions.

National responses can be effective, and normalise the concept of parenting support which may increase engagement with the intervention; however, it is difficult to truly evaluate the effect, and conduct a cost analysis which incorporates evidence of family learning. The Baby Box is an example of early intervention which is targeted to vulnerable families by generic promotion throughout the population of all new parents. Interpretation of research data has to consider mitigating circumstances of an intervention. Participants, who exist in a context of poverty and adversity, may equate submission of positive responses in data with ongoing receipt of goods.

Facilitating active family learning

Play at Home was introduced to the United Kingdom in 1999 (NHS Scotland, 1999). It is a physical activity parenting programme which was initially used within New Zealand in 1990 for parents and children from birth to five years. This intervention is a based upon learning through role-modelling by a professional within the home environment, and aims to increase parent–child interaction. Direct implementation of programmes by facilitators can be responsive to individual needs and circumstances of families. Face-to-face delivery can promote sustainability of the outcomes of an intervention through positive feedback to the parent, and affirmation of the development of parenting skills alongside informational, instrumental, emotional, and social support.

The advent of nursery provision in the 1970s in the United Kingdom responded to children in need, for example in a context of child protection, or parents who required childcare in order to sustain employment. Ironically both sets of circumstances often resulted in weak professional–parent links due to non-availability of primary carers. Nurseries began to develop as family services, and today's settings provide flexible childcare in response to individual circumstances. Family services are traditionally based upon a professional–parent partnership, and develop innovative approaches to engage parents in their children's care and education in the period from six weeks to five years.

Example from practice

Steve takes his daughter, Rosie, to nursery at 7.30 am before boarding the underground train for his work in the city centre. Steve's wife, Lulu, is an accountant. As her job is desk based, Lulu uses e-links to maintain communication with the nursery during each working day. 8 am – Lulu logs into the nursery system to access the latest blog which promotes a review of CCTV parent–child links in UK nurseries. Lulu forwards a text to her husband and highlights the information. 11 am – an email pings onto the computer screen and advertises the nursery newsletter – a quick read gives Lulu an update on eco-activities, healthy eating,

14 *Families and the earliest years*

and the monthly curricular theme. 12 am – Lulu eats a desk lunch and scans the nursery daily photoshoot, seeking out reassurance that her daughter is actively participating in learning. Another e-link for Steve. 3 pm – a text from nursery key worker detailing Rosie's 'achievement of the day', and referring Lulu to the photoshoot gallery.

Electronic media have provided parents with an active and timely link to their children during periods of separation in the early years. This communication system maintains contact between a working parent, and service delivery by secondary attachment figures, but excludes direct links to the child which support social and emotional development.

Child protection projects an expectation of change and development upon a parent, and evidence is sought from outcomes which relate to primary carer and child. It is well known that children are motivated to seek out learning which is based upon their interests and skills, and the same principles apply to adult learners.

Example from practice

Lorna's son, Mark, is two years and three months old. Lorna always knows Mark's exact chronological age as she regularly attends meetings in a context of child protection. Stating personal details of a child quickly and competently in the Sheriff court, Children's Panel Meetings, or Core Groups is a parent's initial claim to be considered as "a significant person" in the child's future. Lorna has been referred to our service for the development of parenting skills. This teenage mother is well known to the service as she also attended throughout her childhood. Lorna's status changed in the earliest years of her life: a child on the child protection register, a child who was looked after by the local authority in loco parentis, a child who experienced supervised or unsupervised (for a short period) access visits with her mother or father, a teenage care-leaver entering adulthood, a teenage care-leaver who was vulnerable due to pregnancy, a single teenage parent and care-leaver under 25 years of age – eligible to access extended support from the local authority.

As Lorna completed an application form for Mark's nursery placement, I observed that her writing was neat, uniform, and the information was recorded with confidence. In the initial stages of professional–parent relationships, particularly in circumstances of parenting within a legal framework, it is essential to capitalise on skills and interests of parents. Lorna's involvement with the service rapidly became engagement as the team planned, and negotiated a programme of learning in which she could demonstrate artistic talents, and personal attainment in addition to contributing to the service. Certificates, videos, and photographs provided media in which to recognise and celebrate the tiny steps to Lorna's development as a responsive parent, and for this vulnerable young adult to gain an understanding of her sense of self.

What does this mean in theory and practice?

- The role of helper can support development of empathy from parent to child.
- The use of empathy can result in an increase in understanding of behaviour and outcomes for self and others.
- The role of helper can support a change in perceptions which directly impacts upon behaviour, actions, and emotions of a parent.
- A change in perceptions can support development of the theory of mind.
- The theory of mind is a significant factor in a process of change.

Braun, Davis, and Mansfield (2006) presented a conceptual understanding of change and development in this context through a theoretical framework based upon a Family Partnership Model, which has a core principle of helping. The authors promoted that adoption of the helper role activated skills which supported learning for a developing person, in this example, a parent. It is interesting to note that Braun et al. acknowledge fluidity within this theoretical model.

Voluntary sector

The "helping model" has been used for many years within the voluntary (third) sector and relates directly to the composition of voluntary organisations, and expectations regarding service provision and service delivery. The voluntary sector services are based upon principles that the service will be immersed within a community and respond to specific cultural needs at local level. Also, strategy and operations will be actioned by or in agreement with community representatives. Voluntary sector funding is short term, and rarely linked to mainstream funding. The short-term nature of projects has been complimented by availability of training for third-sector employees over a range of disciplines. Employees can access generic local authority professional development opportunities, and the voluntary sector workforce can also participate in training by health, education, and social work. Additionally, there are many in-service opportunities which are often delivered in an integrated context by other third-sector providers.

The voluntary sector workforce acquires a broad base of professional knowledge, and practical expertise which includes specialist skills in relation to a particular organisation, or cultural need in an area. Financial constraints in recent years within the public sector have unexpectedly created opportunities for promotion of the third-sector role, in partnership with mainstream services. Funding for pilot interventions may have a duration of six to 18 months as opposed to previous terms of three to five years. It can be challenging for mainstream providers to release a member of staff for a short period in order to conduct a pilot project, for example, diverting a social worker or health visitor from a case load, or teacher from a classroom, could potentially impact upon the core service. Short-term posts are difficult to back-fill with experienced practitioners and tend to attract newly qualified workers or probationers.

A common feature of voluntary sector funding is the delivery of short-term projects; therefore, allocation of roles and delegation of responsibilities can be managed within this organisational context without weakening the core service. The voluntary sector has recently been given opportunities to implement and to evaluate programmes linked to government research. These processes have raised the profile of this sector in practice, publications, and formal/informal presentation of information in relation to the outcomes (Scottish Government, 2017b). If a pilot project is adopted by a government for national use, or a local authority in response to a particular need, then the third-sector workforce will take a key role in training and supporting mainstream services.

Financial constraints in service delivery can be challenging and appear prohibitive to optimum care; however, in a context of integrated working, innovative and unexpected results can be achieved, and partnerships forged, which are based upon an increase in understanding. A recent review of social work systems and practices in England and Wales (McNeish, Sebba, Luke, and Rees, 2017) referred to financial constraints in current delivery of services, and suggested a potential route to increase resources as the use of non-social work professionals within the core teams. Professionals are the active agents who initiate closure of the implementation gap in services by developing the application of knowledge in practice due to an increase in understanding.

The helping model, within this sector, refers to professionals and parents assuming reciprocal roles in which they are *helping*, and *being helped*, by using personal/professional expertise to benefit self, the wider organisation, and community. The process of using latent skills and interests provides opportunities for parents to feel empowered in the early stages of involvement with services. Learning which is based upon experiential practice supports development of the five stages which lead to the autobiographical self.

Gaps in these stages of development can be supported through intervention in adulthood.

Stages of self

The context of *family learning* provides ideal circumstances for parents, as a child's primary carers, to gain insight into their own development of self in addition to nurturing their child's autobiographical self.

1 **Physical agent** – my physical world
2 **Social agent** – my social world
3 **Teleological agent** – understanding *and* applying knowledge of cause/effect
4 **Intentional mental agent** – understanding my impact upon the world
5 **Autobiographical self** – ready to learn

An understanding of self is a necessary component to consolidate or to reform the inner model, and an integral part of individuality (Trevarthan and Aitken, 2001). Interpretation of the world and subsequent comprehension links to actions and emotions forming an *experience*. The inner working model is created by an accumulation of experiences pre-birth, and post-birth throughout the lifespan. This reference framework sorts and compartmentalises experiential learning during waking and sleeping periods. High emotional wellbeing, and motivation to learn, support an individual to review this reference framework in a context of change and potential reconfiguration. Questioning previous comprehension, and associated actions and emotions, is the pathway to development.

A chaotic environment may not promote factors which are conducive to development of a sense of self. An example was highlighted within a recent longitudinal study by Enlow, Egeland, Blood, Wright, and Wright (2012). Data from 206 children were analysed to explore a link between inter-personal trauma exposure in infancy and cognitive development. Findings indicated that this specific type of trauma produced adverse effects which persisted into late childhood.

Fischer and Bidell (2006) linked a weak comprehension of the autobiographical self to difficulties in demonstrating social and emotional reciprocity which posed a potential barrier to the creation and maintenance of relationships as an adult. This process of reconstruction of the inner representation of the world in childhood can impact upon responses in adulthood (Braun et al., 2006). For example, comprehension which is gained from social referencing in childhood may be retained, and it may result in a stimulus response in adulthood within a similar context.

18 *Families and the earliest years*

Developmental gaps

Interactive parenting work, in a context of child protection with several generations vividly exposes *developmental gaps* in construction of the autobiographical self for grandparents, parents, and children. Miell (1995) described the average five-year-old child as having comprehension of a sense of the autobiographical self.

Family interventions are based upon empowerment, learning, and upskilling. It is essential that facilitators understand and respond to these developmental gaps. Each practitioner is bound to practice within an organisational pedagogy, and by using interventions which are deemed appropriate by government, local authority, or individual services. Interventions provide a framework, and media to impart knowledge, understanding, and to initiate a process of change which leads to effective parenting. Facilitators should maintain a focus on the complexities of human development and the unique responses by each parent and child, separately and during parent–child interaction, in the context of family learning. Reflection upon the minutiae associated with change and development provides a rich source of learning for the facilitator which supports programme implementation, and clarifies the links between theory, guidance, and practice.

Vulnerable parents who are operating within child protection processes often represent a second generation of the family supported by local authority care. The parents' primary carers, who are frequently granted the status of kinship carers for their grandchildren, are the first generation. Several generations of families may reside in one local area, and attend a long-standing service for support. I am currently working with extended families of three generations within a context of child protection, and this is a common feature of services today.

Change and development in human beings does not occur within a fixed timescale, although interventions tend to be time limited, including the evaluation of outcomes for funders. Family learning is inter-generational, and short-term progress can be imperceptible. It is important to view the child and parents within his or her family circumstances, and to identify evidence of change which may reflect engagement with the process prior to achieving the expected outcome. For example, a subtle and obvious change in a parent's perceptions should be re-affirmed by the practitioner to the parent, in addition to development of his or her understanding of self which encompasses theory of mind. Self-recognition of achievement can be encouraged by a practitioner noticing and reflecting upon progress. This pathway can support parents to scaffold knowledge, and extend their inherent and acquired skills, and to realise their potential to apply knowledge to a range of circumstances. This process is firmly embedded within the role and responsibilities of a responsive parent.

Example from practice

Shelley and I attend a child protection Children's Panel, and we meet the following morning to discuss the action plan. We agree that the atmosphere was tense, the "room was full of professionals," historical issues were re-visited yet again, and achievement of the action plan seemed ambitious within the allocated timescale. Shelley and I look at one another across the table. We review the issues from two different perspectives: Shelley is a mother whose child is accommodated – I am the practitioner with responsibility for putting the decisions into actions.

It is always useful to meet with parents as soon as possible in the aftermath to a panel meeting or attendance at court. Emotional reactions need to be absorbed through a timetable of small steps to achievement of a mandatory outcome. The outcome is mandatory in the sense that it incorporates this mother's only goal – the right to parenting.

Shelley had arrived an hour late to our first pre-arranged meeting, but I praised her effort and thanked her for attending. As a professional, it is challenging to understand the perspective of a parent in Shelley's circumstances.

The following day, she arrives on time and gives me eye contact as we meet. I affirm her commitment through the use of descriptive praise, "Well done Shelley, I can see that you are motivated – you've come on time – you look positive and ready to learn – change is already occurring. You can do this." Positivity and belief from service-provider to service-user is essential and infectious!

Deep-level learning

Laevers (2015) differentiates between two categories of learning: superficial learning, which does not change a child's competencies, and according to Laevers has little relevance to real life, and deep-level learning, which involves the use of stimuli to construct reality and support development.

All human beings will learn at a *sensory level* in relation to opportunities within the proximal (immediate) environment. Humans have an inherent instinct to focus upon close stimulus to the human body, and to activate basic exploration by using their senses. This sensory level equates to superficial learning as termed by Laevers, and children can apply this level of learning within daily living albeit as a demonstration of an immature instinctive reaction to environmental stimuli. A child's use of sensory learning in isolation indicates a low level of functioning. *Deep-level learning* involves a child, parent, or professional, merging *three different sources* of knowledge and understanding which results in *executive functioning* and *actualisation of potential*.

Academic concepts contribute to knowledge within research, but the use of these unfamiliar terms can be a barrier, or even a direct negative impact upon learning within practice. I have often presented to workers in early years, health, and education who have baulked at the use of conceptual terms in training, and described a resultant feeling of uncertainty and challenge to their professional expertise. I find it is useful to quickly follow-up theory with common examples from the field in order to support comprehension of concepts. This approach can be liberating and empowering to practitioners, and insert realism and insight to the understanding of researchers.

The three sources of knowledge and understanding which contribute to deep-level learning are

1 *Sensory learning* from the proximal environment – PRESENT.
2 *Memory-initiated learning* from previous experiences which led to knowledge *and* understanding – PAST.
3 *Extrapolative learning* by using imaginative skills and creation to extend learning opportunities – FUTURE.

Example from practice

1 Sensory learning from the proximal environment.

Colin is participating in a nursery session with his daughter, Mandy. She is three years old and demonstrates a passion for home-play activities. Today Colin and Mandy are next to the water tray. Colin is crouched on a nursery chair, and Mandy leans against her father as they review the water toys – the water is clear with a few stray bubbles of soap around the edges of the tray; there are two dolls sitting upright with hands outstretched, two little jugs, and two multi-holed flower pots float towards Mandy. Colin offers a handful of soap bubbles to Mandy to smell, then he washes the dolls' hands, and suggests that Mandy creates more bubbles by using the flower pots to stir the water. The little girl splashes and laughs as father and daughter make eye contact, smiling and celebrating this shared time together.

Example from practice

1 Sensory learning from the proximal environment
2 Memory-initiated learning from previous experiences which led to knowledge *and* understanding

Four-year-old Alessandra and her mother Agata are sitting on green and pink beanbags. Alessandra is still settling into nursery and seeks reassurance from her mother's presence. The key worker has prompted Agata to initiate interaction with her daughter using the stacking dolls, Alessandra's current favourite activity. Alessandra focuses upon pulling the dolls quickly apart and dropping the pieces onto the beanbags, ensuring that the activity can be completed near her mother. Agata encourages Alessandra to match the same sizes and shapes through role-modelling. Key worker intervenes and gently says to the little girl, "You can do it, remember (pointing to her head) you played yesterday with these dolls with your friend, Sophie, remember Sophie matched the red doll and you matched the yellow doll . . . ." Alessandra stood up, retrieved the two yellow halves, achieved her goal, and said to the key worker, "I did it!"

Example from practice

1 Sensory learning from the proximal environment
2 Memory-initiated learning from previous experiences which led to knowledge *and* understanding
3 Extrapolative learning by using imaginative skills and creation to extend learning opportunities

Sia and her three-year-old son Kimi are faced with a problem. They are sitting with legs outstretched on a soft fluffy rug in the nursery book corner. Kimi has planned to build a tower of wooden bricks, but the uneven rug surface is causing his tower to collapse. . . .

Sia and Kimi exchange glances and rueful smiles as the tower tumbles once more. They converse in Mandarin. Kimi nods excitedly at his mum, looks around the playroom, and spots a flat box lid which he quickly transports to the book corner. A few moments later and success – plan, implement, reflect, re-configure, and goal achievement. The tower is splendid, balanced safely on the box lid.

Effective practice involves the creation of a therapeutic relationship (Rogers, 1990) to promote a high level of involvement, wellbeing, and secure attachment. The outcome is executive functioning and actualisation of potential: an individual will have the ability, through deep-level learning, and the capacity, through high emotional wellbeing, to demonstrate knowledge and skills in purposeful activity.

Theory of mind

Learning through reflection is increasingly recognised as a mechanism for change. Interventions are based upon the premise that greater reflective functioning by a parent leads to an increase in ability (intellectual), and capacity (emotional wellbeing) to understand the impact of one's own actions and the actions of others: the theory of mind.

Comprehension of the theory of mind is a significant developmental stage for a human being to operate effectively within a social society. Cicchetti and Toth (2006) described the process as a shift from situation-based to representation-based understanding of behaviour.

The following aspects are outcomes from comprehension of the theory of mind.

- Ability (intellectual) and capacity (emotional wellbeing) to self-regulate actions – what you do
- Knowledge and understanding of the link between actions and behaviour – for self and others
- The ability to differentiate and to understand emotions – emotional literacy
- Capacity to demonstrate empathic responding – understanding and reflecting upon the perceptions of others

A recent example of this approach in the United Kingdom is a project called "Minding the Baby" based upon a US model (Grayton, Burns, Pistrang and Fearon, 2017). It is described as a mentalisation-based preventative parenting programme which promotes secure attachment through an increase in parental reflective functioning. This intervention is targeted towards parents under 25 years of age who have additional and complex learning needs. A practitioner will role-model good parenting practices within the familiar microsystem of the home. This facilitator will set daily tasks which are distinctly relevant to the needs of each family, and parents will be encouraged and expected to *practice* their parenting skills. The next step for development is discussion which includes reflection on actions and behaviour in order to extract detailed explanation of the implementation of the daily tasks. The result of this mentalisation-based approach is an increase in understanding of parent–child attachment, and positive or negative interactions upon development.

Family learning values

Eight values underpin the National Occupational Standards for family learning (Scottish Government, 2016):

1 A parent is primary educator.
2 Family learning is inclusive and offered to parents through open access.
3 Family learning processes value and respect diversity of culture, race, relationships, and beliefs.
4 Implementation is based upon equal professional–parent partnerships.
5 Family learning recognises that "making and understanding mistakes" is encompassed within reflective learning.
6 Family learning empowers communities through change.
7 Family learning raises aspirations, and all outcomes are granted equal importance.
8 Family learning operates within a culture of mutual respect for individuals, communities, colleagues, and organisations.

What does this mean in theory and practice?

Two theories can be used to support understanding of family learning by focusing upon the professional–parent relationship (Rogers, 1990) and the process of learning (Magnusson and Stattin, 2006).

The first theory focuses upon the professional–parent relationship. The six necessary conditions for the creation of a therapeutic relationship by Rogers (1990) continue to be applicable to the context of family learning, and support implementation of these values in practice.

The Therapeutic Alliance:

1 **A parent and professional in psychological contact.**

   Psychological contact is different to a relationship in which only information is exchanged. In this specific context of psychological contact, the professional and parent create a dyad – a unit of two people who have a shared focus. There is an expectation by both parties that information will be exchanged in the form of knowledge, there will be reciprocal interaction, and learning will occur by the *developing person*, the parent, achieving an increase in understanding which supports a process of change.

2 **The parent is vulnerable.**

   Human beings experience a sensitive period for learning which is associated with parenthood, particularly in the early stages of pregnancy and post-birth. The plasticity of the human brain enables learning to occur relatively easily during sensitive periods; however vulnerability of the parent means that he or she is receptive to positive and negative influences. The parent's inner working model may be changed in this time which incorporates his or her interpretation of the world, perceptions, actions, behaviour, and emotions associated with parental responsibilities.

3   **The professional is demonstrating resilience.**

The role of professional in family learning exposes a worker to the emotions of a parent and child. In order for a professional to actively demonstrate resilience to the effect of this emotional output, he or she has to create links between his or her actions, behaviour, and emotions, and gain support from bureaucracy, and peers.

4   **The professional showsrespect/non-judgemental responses.**

Self-awareness, self-critique, and reflection are essential elements to achieve optimum practice as a professional.

5   **The professional is able to view the world from the parent's perspective and to communicate this understanding.**

The professional develops the skill of transference in order to truly understand the parent's perspective and to respond effectively.

6   **Any indication of empathy and positive regard contributes to creation of a therapeutic relationship.**

Rogers appreciated that a therapeutic relationship can occur accumulatively, within the context of multiple psychological contexts. A minimal level of empathy and regard can be positive factors in the creation of this relationship.

The second theory focuses upon the process of learning. The three principles of novelty, pleasure, and reality are regarded as integral to change and development (Magnusson and Stattin, 2006).

The Social-Address Model:

- The *principle of novelty* is described as a human being's inherent desire to seek out, and to embrace new experiences.
- The *principle of pleasure* relates to a positive experience, often relating to a personal interest, which leads to an increase in knowledge and understanding of the world.
- The *principle of reality* supports application of this newly acquired comprehension of the world, and potential re-configuration of the inner working model.

Example from practice

It is nearly pick-up time in nursery. The noise level has subsided as the 2–3 year old children are tired, and ready to go home for lunch. Some children are playing, some are listening for the entry buzzer to indicate that a parent is arriving. I notice that Carlo is standing still, a yellow Lego brick in one hand, the other hand resting on the wooden table which is strewn with different sizes of Lego constructions, and train tracks as created by his peers throughout the morning session.

Carlo's dad, Pedro, enters the playroom. Pedro works shifts and rarely attends nursery to collect his son – I notice that he is uncomfortably aware of workers watching, and potentially assessing his parental actions. I beckon to Pedro and indicate that he sits beside me on a nursery chair. Nursery chairs are designed well by manufacturers to embrace the weight of an adult. Health and safety excludes adult chairs in a child-friendly environment, but a parent sitting on a nursery chair can easily view the world from the perspective of a child.

I observe Pedro beginning to relax as he picks up some toys to create foot-space for his large black safety boots. Pedro retrieves two Lego bricks and automatically locks one to the other. Every adult can remember, and re-enact vivid memories of childhood activities. A nursery ambience ignites the childlike qualities in parents, and Pedro gained confidence as he looked at me expectantly, waiting, and wondering.

I point to Carlo, and explain to Pedro that his little boy is actively "problem solving" – an extremely important stage of cognitive development. Pedro mirrors my excitement and grins proudly. Carlo is regulating his actions, reflecting, planning, and creating a Lego masterpiece. Pedro leans forward and commences his own Lego plan – father and son compete for a few moments, then cooperate in choices of yellow or red bricks. Family learning . . . .

What does this mean in theory and practice?

- Pedro's own childhood interests have been activated by this spontaneous opportunity to participate in his son's learning (principle of novelty).
- Pedro gains satisfaction and an outcome of achievement from cooperative play with Carlo (principle of pleasure).
- Pedro is fascinated by gaining insight into the complexity of brain development as illustrated by this simple interaction with his little son (principle of reality).

The next chapter explores family learning in practice and links the concept to inclusion.

References

Bowlby, J. (1979). *The making and breaking of affectional bonds*. Abingdon: Routledge.
Boxford, S., King, Y., Irani, M., Spencer, H., Bridger-Wilkinson, E., Barker, S., Hill-Dixon, A., and Cordis Bright (2017). *Evaluation of the family learning intervention programme. Research report 27*. London: Department for Education.
Braun, D., Davis, H., and Mansfield, P. (2006). *How helping works: Towards a shared model of process*. London: The Centre for Parent and Child Support.
Bronfenbrenner, U. (1979). *The ecology of human development* (2nd edition). Cambridge, MA: Harvard University Press.
Bronfenbrenner, U. (2005). *Making human beings human*. Thousand Oaks, CA: Sage.
Cara, O., and Brooks, G. (2012). *Evidence of the wider benefits of family learning: A scoping review*. Research paper number 93. London: Department for Business, Innovation & Skills.
Cicchetti, D., and Toth, S. L. (2006). Developmental psychopathology and preventive intervention. In W. Damon and R. Lerner (Eds.), *Handbook of child psychology* (volume 4, pp. 511–512). Hoboken, NJ: John Wiley & Sons.
Dalli, C. (2014). *Quality for babies and toddlers in early years' settings*. Occasional paper 4, Association for the Professional Development of Early Years' Educators. TACTYC, London.
Department for Children, Schools and Families. (2009). *Social work task force*. Retrieved 1 December 2009, from www.dcsf.gov.uk/swtf/
Department for Education and Skills. (2004). *The effective provision of pre-school education (EPPE) project: The final report*. Nottingham: The Institute of Education.
Enlow, M. B., Egeland, B., Blood, E., Wright, R. O., and Wright, R. J. (2012). *Interpersonal trauma exposure and cognitive development in children to age 8 years: A longitudinal study*. Retrieved 17 April 2012, from http://jech.bmj.com/content/early/2012/03/22/jech-2011-200727
Fischer, K. W., and Bidell, T. R. (2006). The bioecological model of human development. In W. Damon and R. M. Lerner (Eds.), *Handbook of child psychology* (volume 1, p. 377). Hoboken, NJ: Wiley & Sons.
Grayton, L., Burns, P., Pistrang, N., and Fearon, P. (2017). *Minding the baby, qualitative findings on implementation from the first UK service*. London: National Society for the Protection of Cruelty to Children (NSPCC).
Harris, A., and Goodall, J. (2007). *Engaging parents in raising achievement: Do parents know they matter?* Research report DCSF-RW004. London: Department for Children, Schools & Families.
Harvard Family Research Project. (2006). *Family involvement in early childhood*. Briefing number 1. Retrieved 6 April 2017, from www.hfrp.org
Heckman, J. L. (2011). *The economics of inequality*. Retrieved 2 July 2017, from http://ftp.iza.org/dp3515.pdf
HM Government. (2008a). *The early years' foundation stage*. Retrieved 2 July 2017, from www.legislation.gov.uk/uksi/2008/1743//contents/made
HM Government. (2008b). *Common assessment framework*. London: Department of Children, Schools & Families.

HM Government. (2008c). *Common core of skills and knowledge for the children's workforce*. London: Department for Education & Schools.
HM Government. (2012). *The early years' foundation stage*. Retrieved 2 July 2017, from www.legislation.gov.uk/uksi/2012/2463/contents/made
HM Government. (2014). *Children and families act 2014*. Retrieved 2 July 2017, from www.legislation.gov.uk/ukpga.2014/6/contents/enacted
Joseph, S. (2015). *Positive therapy, building bridges between positive psychology and person-centred psychotherapy* (2nd edition). Hove: Routledge.
Laevers, F. (2015). *Making care and education more effective through wellbeing and involvement: An introduction to experiential education*. Belgium: Centre for Experiential Education.
Lamberton, L., Devaney, J., and Bunting, L. (2016). New challenges in family support: The use of digital technology in supporting parents. *Child Abuse Review*. Retrieved 9 March 2017, from http://onlinelibrary.com.doi/10.1002/car.2451/abstract;jsessionid=A1F12B4592
Lee, P. (2008). Social capital, families & community learning & development. *Scottish Youth Issues Journal, number 11*. Bristol: Policy Press.
Magnusson, D., and Stattin, H. (2006). The person in context: A holistic-interactionist approach. In W. Damon and R. Lerner (Eds.), *Handbook of child psychology* (volume 1, pp. 400–410, 418–424, 433). Hoboken, NJ: John Wiley & Sons.
McNeish, D., Sebba, J., Luke, N., and Rees, A. (2017). *What have we learned about good social work systems and practice?* Oxford: Department for Education.
Miell, D. (1995). The development of self. In P. Barnes (Ed.), *Personal, social and emotional development of children* (pp. 190–201). Blackwell: Open University.
Moran, P., Ghate, D., and van der Merwe, A. (2004). *What works in parenting support? A review of the international evidence*. London: Department for Education and Skills.
National Institute of Adult Continuing Education (NIACE). (2013). *Family learning works, the inquiry into family learning in England and Wales*. Retrieved 6 April 2017, from http://shopniace.org.uk/media/ctalog/product/n/i/niacefamilylearningreportreprintfinal.pdf
The National Parent Forum of Scotland. (2017). *Review of the impact of the Scottish schools (parental involvement) act 2006*. Edinburgh: Scottish Government.
NHS Scotland. (1999). *Play at home*. Retrieved 15 July 2017, from www.parentingacrossscotland.org/info-for-families/resources/play-home-nhs-health-
Nurture Network. (2017). *Nurture portrait 2015–16, a snapshot of the social, emotional and behavioural difficulties in pupils throughout the UK*. Retrieved 6 April 2017, from www.nurturinggroups.org
Rogers, C. (1990). *The Carl Rogers reader*. Cornwall: MPG Books Ltd.
Save the Children. (2013). *Too young to fail*. Retrieved 6 April 2017, from www.savethechildren.org.uk/sites/default/files/images/TooYoungToFailO.pdf
Scottish Government. (2006). *Scottish schools (parental involvement) act 2006*. Edinburgh: Scottish Government.
Scottish Government. (2008a). *Family learning within the early years' framework*. Retrieved 4 June 2017, from www.gov.scot/Publications/2008/06/family-learning
Scottish Government. (2008b). *The early years' framework*. Edinburgh: Scottish Government.

28 Families and the earliest years

Scottish Government. (2012). *National parenting strategy – Making a positive difference to children and young people through parenting.* Edinburgh: Scottish Government.

Scottish Government. (2014). *The children and young peoples' (Scotland) act 2014.* Edinburgh: Scottish Government.

Scottish Government. (2016). *Review of family learning, supporting excellence and equity.*Edinburgh: Scottish Government.

Scottish Government. (2017a). *Scotland's baby box pilot research.* Edinburgh: Scottish Government.

Scottish Government. (2017b). *Mental health strategy: 2017–2027.* Edinburgh: Scottish Government.

Siraj-Blatchford, I., Sylva, K., Muttock, S., Gilden, R., and Bell, D. (2002). *Researching effective pedagogy in the early years.* Report number 356 (pp. 8, 11, 32, 98–102, 133–135, 141). London: Department for Education and Skills.

Trevarthan, C., and Aitken, K. J. (2001). Infant intersubjectivity: Research, theory, and clinical applications. *Journal of Child Psychology and Psychiatry, volume 42.* Cambridge: Cambridge University Press.

Van Houte, S., Bradt, L., Vandenbroeck, M., and Bouverne-De Bie, M. (2013). Professionals' understanding of partnership with parents in the context of family support programmes. *Journal of Child and Family Social Work.* Oxford: Blackwell Publishing.

Whitters, H. G. (2009). *Parents and an integrated team: Developing and maintaining effective relationships to support early interventions.* Glasgow: Strathclyde University Library.

2 Special needs to inclusion

Professional development

Practitioners will be familiar with the expression *managing children's behaviour*. It is often used as a title for in-service training courses. Training topics for continuous professional development (CPD) are chosen for impact value. In-service days are given high regard by practitioners and organisations, and allocated training topics are elevated significantly within the context of organisational pedagogy. Practitioners will freely discuss the topic in advance of in-service training, sharing knowledge, agreeing, and disagreeing, accessing information which is gleaned from previous employment or perhaps the media, checking the organisation's stance on issues, and pre-empting challenges which might be presented during training. In-service foci tend to be raised in the media due to their topicality for example current United Kingdom issues are the national review into historical childhood abuse, inclusion, and standardised testing of attainment.

Pre-training discussions by a team can often result in acquisition of a group attitude, and interpretation of an issue which may need to be challenged during training. Informal peer professional development interactions, for example discussion in a staff-room, can be directed by a staff member who is adept at promoting opinion from a personal perspective, as opposed to an informed professional base. I always spend the first few minutes of training sessions exploring personal versus professional attitudes and beliefs on the topic.

In-service training is mandatory in relation to accumulation of CPD for professional registration. An in-service day provides a welcome oasis of calm within busy workplaces. Staff will look forward to a working day without tight parameters: perhaps an hour for lunch, several tea breaks, dress-down day, fewer phone calls, choosing which e-mails to open, going home a little earlier! It is easy to embrace new knowledge in this environment. It is easy to be generous to colleagues by listening carefully to ideas and explanations. It is easy to convince yourself that you can adapt and learn.

The day after in-service training, we enter our services with positivity laced by an increase in comprehension; however a working environment directs our practice through regular prompts and signals which lead to familiar thought processes, the implementation of tried and tested routines, and reactions with little scope for the influx of *new* ideas. Post-training analysis requires the practitioner to present detailed comprehension of an issue by recording the learning that has been acquired, proposed practice in the workplace, and outcome for service-users and self. Follow-up monitoring by senior staff is necessary and essential to ensure that research and theory have a long-term impact upon the implementation of service.

Knowledge and understanding

It is straightforward to transfer knowledge from one medium to another. Knowledge can be *cut and paste* to inform legislation, national guidance, local authority policy, organisational policy, and ultimately the practitioner who works directly with parent and child. Knowledge is weak unless it is accompanied by understanding. An increase in understanding requires complex processes to occur within an individual. Knowledge is acquired and interpreted in the context of an inner working model – unique to each human being. Interpretation leads to formulation of perceptions and beliefs influenced by personal, family, community, and professional culture. Perceptions activate emotions and associative behaviour. Skills are consolidated or re-formed. Neural pathways are created or strengthened in the brain, and development occurs.

Sharing an increase in understanding is a separate skill to gaining comprehension for your own development needs. The expertise of a trainer lies in his or her ability to impart understanding which leads to deep-level learning for each recipient. Titles of modules are the responsibility of trainers, and they present an immediate message to learners regarding their position of power in a context of working with families. This is an important feature in the delivery of knowledge. For example, degree and diploma courses have generally updated modular titles on behaviour, and frequently describe course content as "promoting positive behaviour" as opposed to traditional "managing negative behaviour". Course leaders are well aware that students learn from subtleties in communication within a year group, in addition to formal peer review and feedback. Students in a cohort maintain contact with one another through texting to individuals, to a specific group or the entire student population. Implications are embedded in texts, and this medium of communication is another example of a potential source which influences attitudes and beliefs during the uptake of knowledge for professionals.

It is easy for us to claim that our comprehension has been increased after training. Evaluation materials relating to course delivery and content promote expectations of achievement; however, registration requires workers to have professional integrity. Honest self-reflection, self-critique, and self-evaluation are necessary techniques to use in affirming professional development.

Reflection

Practice approaches are based upon knowledge, understanding and expectations of society within a particular period of time, and these invariably change. Expectations are bound and liberated by policies and procedures. Reflection is a useful tool and currently a popular medium for learning; however practitioners may confuse reflection with hindsight.

- *Hindsight* contributes a superficial level of understanding. It is based upon the use of evidence from an outcome to justify or to criticise actions.
- *Reflection* gives clarity to actions, post-event, by extracting understanding and applying this insight to development of the professional self and practice.

The collegiate aspect of work teams can be affected by self-critique or criticism of previous practice as highlighted by workers of different ages and stages in their careers. Learning in any professional discipline is accumulative, and the initial foundation is strengthened over time by using a cyclical approach of knowledge acquisition, an increase in comprehension, reflection, and refining through consolidation or extension. The vocational career of the early years' practitioner is stimulating, challenging, exacting, and fulfilling due to change, and deeper insight into the complexities of human development.

Sensitive periods for learning

Our understanding of the process of learning has been enriched largely due to the input from neuroscience and acknowledgement of the emotional needs of children in a context of attachment. Society's expectations have changed too, and educators uphold the rights of individuals in addition to social groups. Today's practitioners confidently and competently discuss brain architecture, secure and insecure attachment, and environmental influences. Several periods in the lifespan have been identified as sensitive for learning: pre-birth to three years, adolescence, and the stage in which an adult becomes a parent. The term adolescence has been adopted recently to represent the years of puberty, 10–25 years, which was formerly known as the teenage years, 13–19. Puberty can commence at 10 years, and the brain continues to grow until 25 years of age. The brain is genetically programmed to be particularly receptive to recognising and embracing learning opportunities during these times, and this facilitates knowledge acquisition and retention.

Research into brain development is widespread and well-funded in the United Kingdom and elsewhere. Evidence shows that the brain has plasticity and can continue to develop throughout a lifespan by making structural changes in the form of neural pathways, and functional change in the patterns which are created to support executive functioning. For example, the early years' workforce have made these changes during professional development in a context of inclusion and family learning. Operational practices have been adapted and improved due to an increase in understanding of the best approach to optimising care and education for all children. Professional responses will continue to evolve over time.

Legislation

The Salamanca Statement and Framework for Action presented a principle for the promotion of inclusion to countries throughout the world in 1994 (United Nations Educational, Scientific, and Cultural Organisation, 1994). In the United Kingdom, this principle was promoted through legislation in the format of the Education (Additional Support for Learning) (Scotland) Act 2004 and subsequently reviewed in 2009 (Scottish Executive, 2004; Scottish Government, 2009). The Education (Scotland) Act 2016 was implemented this year, 2017. It supports a change to Scottish education in contexts of attainment and additional support for learning needs, and children's rights (Scottish Government, 2016). UK legislation (Department for Children and Schools, 1996, 2001, 2014) includes the Education Act (1996), Special Educational Needs and Disability Act (2001), and more recently the Children and Families Act (2014).

The term *special educational needs* in the UK context was replaced by *additional support for learning needs*. The significance can be missed in relation to this pivotal change as publications often focus upon the change of descriptor as opposed to a change in concept. This new description minimises the use of the term *needs* as a stereotypical label which defined a child. Explanation is represented by wording in the descriptor which recognises the responsibility of services in providing support for a child to learn. Today, children are regarded first and foremost as learners who have the right to education which responds to their personal interpretation of the world.

Executive functioning

Executive functioning is defined as the use of mental processes to purposefully operate in a society (Centre on the Developing Child, 2016). *Purposeful operation* is a descriptor which requires clarification in the context of family learning and inclusion. Executive functioning is achieved as an individual plan, and implements an action which leads to achievement of potential. The action may contribute directly and positively to the proximal or distal environment, and other people within these contexts, *or* the positive contribution can be related to fulfilment of the individual. Personal fulfilment of a child with complex needs does represent purposeful operation in society within the context of inclusion.

Early intervention for families

Governments have responded rapidly through allocation of funding to the early years' sector and training of the workforce. Currently, childcare and education may be promoted within evidence-based parenting programmes (Nursery World, 2016), for example, The Positive Parenting Programme (Triple P), Mellow Parenting, Incredible Years, and Circle of Security, or may be immersed in a specific approach to childcare and education such as Solihull (Solihull Approach Parenting Group Research, 2009). The significant impact from parenting interventions is the application of principles which may be actioned by using different media. Moran, Ghate, and Van der Merwe (2004) conducted an extensive review of parenting programmes by researching 2,000 examples from around the world and findings indicated general principles:

- Ensuring health and safety of child and adult
- Enabling child to explore and learn from a variety of environments
- Creating a secure attachment relationship
- Supporting social interaction
- Promoting a child's self-regulation of behaviour

Consistent implementation

Consistency in the delivery of information over a wide population was an aim of Glasgow City Council in 2009–2012. This goal was actioned by the universal training of 850 professionals from the disciplines of health, education, and social work. Groups of professionals were trained to deliver The Positive Parenting Programme (Triple P) by Sanders (2008) and the Solihull Approach (Solihull Approach Parenting Group Research, 2009). The two approaches involved the creation of a relationship between parent and professional. These two examples of early intervention parenting programmes are supported by international and local systems which reflect the dissemination and predicted application of the information. The importance of the parent–professional relationship is promoted by these two approaches, but the parameters of practice vary.

The process for implementing the Positive Parenting Programme was designed by the Triple P Foundation to ensure effective application of a planned, and regulated, formal multi-level intervention. This medium to disseminate informational and emotional support was developed within the academic setting of Queensland University, Australia, as an intervention to improve the quality and consistency of parenting advice for a large population. The process and outcomes of Triple P can be audited to ensure validity of practice within this international public health model for early intervention.

Alternatively, the Solihull Approach was developed by practitioners from a health visiting team in England (Solihull Approach Parenting Group Research, 2009). This early intervention applies the principles of reciprocity, and reflective responding within practice, in order to promote personalised care to meet the needs of individuals. The approach was initially applicable to a local area, and it was not designed to be promoted to large sections of the population; therefore, it does not contain an auditing mechanism. This is an example of an early interventional programme which has the potential to respond to individual needs and local circumstances. The Solihull Approach is used to inform implementation of the Scottish Practice Model through identification of shared principles: containment, reciprocity, and behaviour management (Cabral, 2014).

The link between dissemination and representation of information was discussed within recent research by Mazzucchelli and Sanders (2010) on the Positive Parenting Programme (Triple P). This research investigated the ability of facilitators to adapt the implementation of the Triple P programme to local and cultural needs throughout the world. The study was prompted by the challenge of ensuring consistency of implementation by 21,000 practitioners, in addition to meeting the needs of populations within 19 countries. Findings indicated that this parenting programme could be successfully transposed between countries and cultures. It seems that the parent– professional relationship is a contributory feature of this adaption in the response to individual and local needs.

Theory to practice

Theory is the richest source of understanding which informs and transforms practice. The use of theory is necessary for development of the workforce and progress in service delivery; however theoretical terms and concepts can create challenges for practitioners in the quest for professional expertise. This chapter presents theory followed by practice examples from the field in order to close the implementation gap from research to practice by describing the minute details in optimisation of learning for all.

Attainment – the heritability system

An example of using theory to support a deeper understanding of practice is consideration of a heritability system as an influence upon development and attainment.

Genetic influences are inherited throughout familial generations, and the effect upon development is termed *heritability*. It is well known that siblings or members of an extended family may react differently to the same influences within the family: for example, a parent's use of drugs, mental health issues, domestic violence, or additional learning needs. Learning and behaviour are influenced by

- *Personal characteristics* of the individual child (internal influence) – genetic heritability and personality.
- *Proximal processes* in the environment around the child (external influences) – within the microsystem.

The difference in reactions of siblings is due to the *joint effect* of influences from personal characteristics, and influences from the proximal environment. The effect impacts upon each child's interpretation of the world and subsequent behaviour.

Variance refers to differences in the development of human beings. Variance is demonstrated through each child's actions, behaviour, and emotions. Bronfenbrenner (2005) described this process as *actualisation* of genetic influences into observable phenomena. Practitioners regularly conduct observations (observable phenomena) of children's play in order to assess, evaluate, and record this information (actualisation) in relation to developmental milestones and curricular outcomes.

Optimum outcome

The parent–professional or parent–child relationship has the potential to optimise conditions which support development by providing a *focus of attention* through formal or informal intervention. Intervention can activate genetic potential and initiate a period of learning; however genetic potential is affected by the child's reaction to influences within his daily living environment, and the outcome is not always optimum development. The actualisation of genetic potential supports a child to have a high level of emotional wellbeing. This status increases the child's ability and capacity to recognise and to access positive influences upon his development. Additionally, this process provides a protective mechanism against negative influences (Bronfenbrenner and Morris, 2006) by supporting a child to consider, and to implement choices as opposed to reactive behaviour.

Ironically plasticity of the human brain is a feature which can *support* or *hinder development* (Bergen and Woodin, 2017). Positive factors promote neural connections which lead to development; however, negative factors can increase vulnerability due to the brain's plasticity and receptivity to any influences – positive or negative.

Example from practice

I meet Matt at the door of our service. We exchange a few words about the security system and crackling intercom, then I proffer a handshake. Matt is surprised but responds. Physical contact, within appropriate social boundaries, is a useful prelude to the creation of a therapeutic relationship. It promotes equality, respect, and acceptance.

As we walk down the long corridor to the meeting room, I turn around to face Matt and continue our social "meeting and greeting". A practitioner who boldly strides in front of a vulnerable parent, and dominates entry into a room, projects power and emphasises the professional domain. These actions are not conducive to the therapeutic relationship, and professional–parent working partnerships.

I quietly usher Matt ahead of me into the parent's room. I offer a choice of hot or cold drinks – Matt shrugs and says, "You choose." This response is common from vulnerable families who are not used to recognising and making choices – it is not a pattern of interaction which exists in their daily lives. It gives me an insight into Matt and his perception of the world.

Matt describes himself as a drug addict, but I immediately interject to change this perception. Matt is first and foremost a father. He also has an addiction. The use of labels should be challenged in the process of change and development with families. Labels have attachments in the form of stereotypical assumptions and behaviours. Matt is focusing upon parenthood.

This father knows his children well, and he competently describes the resilience and achievements (actualisation of genetic potential) of his seven-year-old son in comparison to the acute needs of his little two-year-old. I gently inform Matt that life can be interpreted directly through the eyes of a seven-year-old, whereas a two-year-old reflects a

parent's perceptions, emotions, and reactions – adopting fears, negativity, despair....
   Matt is aware that his children are reacting differently (variance) to the adversities in the family lifestyle. I praise Matt's depth of understanding about his children's needs and acknowledge the difficult circumstances. The process of change has already commenced for this father through the interactive guidance which has occurred within the context of an initial induction meeting. Every opportunity should be capitalised upon. I reassure Matt that his two sons will be supported in accordance with their needs (genetic heritability) and reaction (joint effect) to their father's addiction (influences from proximal processes).

What does this mean in theory and practice?

How do we use interactive guidance to support learning which leads to change and development in parents?

Tiny steps of knowledge *and* understanding are constructed by the professional–parent partnership. Key points are the following:

- Explore inner working model of parent.
- Use past to inform present and future – past experiences provide a base of knowledge and understanding which can create a platform for change or consolidate prior learning.
- Notice and affirm a change in perception, a change in interpretation of the world, a change in actions, a change in behaviour, which equals the foundation of resilience and positive parenting.
- Nurture the seven steps of the Dance of Reciprocity with the parent: initiation, orientation, a state of attention, acceleration, peak of excitement, deceleration, withdrawal, or turning away. These momentary seven steps are apparent within a dyadic relationship (pairing) in which learning is occurring.

An optimum developmental outcome for children can be supported by

- Using the personal characteristics of the individual to support learning and development = personality and interests which activates genetic heritability.

   Practice examples: pre-birth to three – supporting our youngest children, Curriculum for Excellence, Early Years Foundation Stage.

- Improving the quality of proximal processes in the environment, and providing learning opportunities which support lower and higher

38 *Special needs to inclusion*

levels of cognitive functioning in order to respond to brain plasticity, and the cyclical nature of brain growth, equals influences from the microsystem in the form of family learning and input from services.

Practice examples: pedagogy associated with National Practice Models Getting It Right for Every Child, Common Assessment Framework – Every Child Matters.

- Providing learning opportunities which focus upon internal processes, for example, increasing the child's readiness to learn, motivation, self-esteem, self-belief, and resilience to adversity.
- Providing learning opportunities which focus upon external processes, for example, intervention for child and extended family.
- Providing opportunities to repeat learning at different cognitive levels in order to encourage the development of neural pathways.

The outcome will be *elevated developmental functioning* of the child = attainment *and* inclusion. In other words, the child will learn, achieve, be fulfilled, and enjoy a wonderful childhood!

Resilience

Resilience is a current concept which is explored and debated by governments, and practitioners. This section discusses the intricate processes which occur within children during an increase in resilience and focuses upon children who have experienced trauma, and children who have additional support for learning needs.

Abajobir (2017) linked abuse in childhood to a poor quality of life. This maxim remains current to the 21st century, and similar examples can be accessed from the past 60 years. The link provides rationale for the work of the early years' workforce. Increasing the quality of life and supporting each child to achieve potential is a generic outcome for every service. Politicians, professionals, parents, and the general public view child protection from different perspectives, but universally agree upon the same projected outcome. The goal is to facilitate a child's access to, and support for, learning which leads to development and achievement of potential.

Barriers to learning

There are barriers to learning which do not relate directly to the source of adversity, but originate from the *child's reactions to the influences* from the adversity. The rationale to improve the quality of life is founded upon minimising this reaction. A current approach is increasing the child's resilience.

During any discussion on resilience, it is worth giving consideration to your professional belief:

Does resilience relate to instinctive reaction or a conscious process; therefore, can resilience be nurtured?

Rutter (2012) commented that resilience is having a relatively good outcome despite adversities. This suggests that resilience is instinctive and an inherent reaction of a human being to adversities which potentially affect health and wellbeing. McCrory, Gerin, and Viding (2017) described the theory of latent vulnerability and expressed that children adapt to the effects of neglect in order to cope and survive. This is an interesting and valuable point, and promotes a warning to professionals that vulnerability remains potentially hidden, despite a child's apparent resilience and ability to achieve.

It is important that services review the child's needs from a holistic perspective by exploring potential influences, protective factors, and the impact upon vulnerability and ultimately resilience. Research indicates that this process can occur within an educational establishment through the support of an attachment figure, and a predictable and consistent learning environment (Bomber, 2007, 2011). Practice models, for example, Scotland's Getting It Right for Every Child, provide materials to support this level of understanding for practitioners – The Resilience Matrix (Scottish Government, 2008).

I believe that resilience has two different sources which are juxtaposed.

1. The first is resilience at a basic, reactive level which links to the child's inherent ability to move away from adversities which impact, or have the potential to impact, upon physical, intellectual, and emotional wellbeing.

    - Physical wellbeing – A child will access physical skill to move away from an adversity, or to turn aside, or to remove eye contact, or to hide or shut his or her own eyes.
    - Intellectual wellbeing – A child will limit exposure to learning opportunities, which may incur danger, by exploring his or her world at a basic sensory level. He or she will minimise physical movement in the environment, and play with his or her hands kept close to his body.
    - Emotional wellbeing – A child will refrain from forming relationships if his or her social overtures receive negative responses. He or she will turn away from another being, avert eye contact, and maintain an impassive expression which signals his or her reaction to rejection. This status is termed *avoidant attachment*.

40 *Special needs to inclusion*

2   Secondly, I believe that resilience can be nurtured by an attachment figure. This approach entails an uptake of knowledge and understanding which is gained directly from adversities. The process supports re-configuration of the inner working model, and subsequent change in perceptions, actions, behaviour, and emotions. The outcome is the emergence of coping mechanisms, and an operational perspective which includes a desire to actively seek out, and to embrace, learning opportunities.

I shall apply the terms *instinctive resilience,* and *acquired resilience* to represent these two sources of resilience.

Example from practice

Instinctive resilience

Lio is 15 months old. He is beginning to develop a mid-line centre of balance, but his physical development is delayed due to spending long periods of time playing, sleeping, and eating in a buggy. The mid-line position is most effective for learning. Every parent will voice that a "good strong buggy" is an essential piece of equipment for daily family life. A buggy or pushchair is constructed to keep a child safe during journeys in outside terrain – the five-point harness adheres to international standards, and restricts the potential for a child to tumble onto the ground. Families who live in adversity will often use a buggy inappropriately. The mid-line posture is not necessary or achievable as Lio is strapped into his familiar buggy seat, so sitting unsupported on the livingroom floor creates a new challenge for this little boy.

Lio's mother and partner operate in a context of domestic violence. The two familiar adults tower above Lio, rarely presenting at his level of vision. Raised angry voices of these primary carers provide an unpredictable backdrop to his existence. His elementary instinctive attempts to gain eye contact with his mother are disregarded. Lio's stepfather sends negative signals to the child through his aggressive body language.

Lio demonstrates and develops patterns of functioning which relate to **instinctive resilience** *to the environmental and social adversities. He remains vigilant. His body is "on alert". His limited physical skills are utilised to move away from potential harm in the home environment. His social overtures have not been met with positive responses; therefore he limits attention-seeking techniques through instinctive survival strategies. He faces the wall. He hears but does not react to the turmoil behind. He maintains exploration at the basic sensory level to minimise*

Special needs to inclusion 41

his impact upon this world in which the adults behave inconsistently, and adversities cannot be predicted.

What does this mean in theory and practice?
- Lio has developed avoidant attachment.
- Lio's neurological systems are activated to prioritise protection of his health and wellbeing (Cozolino, 2013), as opposed to the creation of relationships.
- Lio maintains an immature level of exploration as a response to the limited learning opportunities, and a need to remain in control of his safety.
- Extending his arms, crawling, and satisfying the motivation to scaffold knowledge is tempered by the instinct to cope and survive.
- Additionally, toxic stress reduces the brain's capacity to develop neural connections and to learn effectively (Cozolino, 2013).

Example from practice

Acquired resilience

Lio has been placed on the child protection register. The development of parenting skills has been recorded as action point one in the Child Protection Plan. Lio's mother, Leanne, and her partner, Sandy, attend the service. I notice their seemingly defensive but understandably nervous presentation, jackets remain fastened in the warm room, each adult firmly holding onto a can of juice, and a mobile phone. The couple perch on the edge of a couch, and the brightly coloured cushions add vibrancy to the tense atmosphere. Soft furnishings are often used in services to present a homely relaxed ambience, but ultimately confidence and acceptance of learning has to evolve from inside each adult.

I thank the couple for attending, and present this session as the first important step to change. I seek out Leanne and Sandy's understanding of parenting by focusing upon their own childhood experiences. The majority of parents in the child protection system were once little boys and girls – confused, scared children embraced by legislation and policies to promote their safety. This couple was no exception. Negative abusive experiences are quickly shared with me as a reason for de-faulting on parenting skills for Lio.

I have always found that childhoods are not "completely negative experiences", and most adults can identify positive aspects which provide a basis for learning and development. Leanne signals the early stage of engagement as she lays down her can of juice and slowly unzips her jacket. She considers my question about memorable people

42 *Special needs to inclusion*

in childhood. *"I always liked my granny Jean."* Sandy does not want to be left out of this revelation, and interrupts, *"I always liked my Auntie Bettsey until she died."*

The door has opened to learning. I demonstrate interest and empathy as I notice that the couple are motivated to talk about these attachment figures. Practical examples are recalled by Leanne and Sandy, and strategic questioning used to further discussion of the key features. Our interactions extract meaning from the couple's memories, and this is used to shape a plan which supports the creation of positive relationships with Lio.

Childhood memories

- *"Always the same approach to greeting me each morning"* – predictable behaviour
- *"Using a soft voice and kind words if I hurt myself"* – showing empathy
- *"Giving me praise and showing an interest in my toys"* – supporting self-worth
- *"Giving me a cuddle if things go wrong"* – nurturing resilience
- *"Telling me how things work, like cars and things in the house"* – scaffolding knowledge
- *"Helping with homework so I don't get in trouble at school"* – unconditional acceptance and love
- *"Giving me a bath and a hug with a dry towel"* – physical and emotional care

We quietly discuss links between actions of adults and emotions of children. We choose two actions to practice with Lio this week. I produce paper and coloured pens for the couple to record a home plan – ownership of change is essential for cooperation of parents in child protection which reduces dependency on services. I detect the rudimentary skills of **acquired resilience** emerging from this couple.

What does this mean in theory and practice?

- The therapeutic relationship between professional and parents is used as a medium to demonstrate empathy, and to transfer knowledge and understanding.
- A demonstration of empathy and positive regard supports the creation and positive effect from a therapeutic relationship (Rogers, 1990).
- Historical influences from the couple's microsystems are being accessed to support a change in the current microsystem.

Special needs to inclusion   43

- The couple are empowered through becoming agents of change and gaining realisation of latent parenting skills.
- Acquired resilience in the primary carers is being nurtured as a first step to an increase in resilience of the child.

Nurturing resilience

Each child's learning needs should be assessed and determined within the context of the professional–parent partnership by pooling these two sources of expertise. Development of resilience requires several conditions. In practice these conditions should be further sub-divided as appropriate to represent the individual needs of every child.

1 A responsive attachment figure
2 A readiness to learn
3 An accessible source of knowledge
4 Emotional literacy
5 Self-regulation

1. A RESPONSIVE ATTACHMENT FIGURE

Over the last 10 years, professionals in early years have received extensive training on attachment, and this knowledge and increase in comprehension of children's emotional needs have contributed positively to practice.

An overview of practice and pedagogy can be gained by listening to and observing daily interactions. I feel that practitioners can misinterpret attachment through over-familiarity with the concept. Terminology has been created and applied in practice which is perceived by practitioners as relating to attachment, but actually demonstrates an implementation gap – knowledge is acquired without understanding. I hear practitioners exchange comments concerning attachment which clearly represents this gap, for example, "Is Tony attached or not? Has Sara managed to get secure attachment yet?"

The creation of a secure relationship is not the responsibility of a child, but it depends on the attachment figure responding to the child's emotional needs. I find that it is useful to add a descriptor to attachment during training or practice, for example, the term *responsive* provides a timely reminder of the responsibility of the adult – parent or practitioner. This prompt refocuses workers to consider the complexity of the neuro-biological and emotional processes associated with secure attachment. For example, Van der Kolk (2003) emphasised the significance of the modulation effect as the responses of an attachment figure increased and decreased stimulus – termed *affect attunement*.

2. A READINESS TO LEARN

Children who operate within a context of adversities instinctively maintain the status quo, and they may not actively seek out, or embrace, learning opportunities. A child who is surrounded by negativity within the home environment, for example, domestic violence, drug use, and mental health of parents, exists in an unpredictable world. The child learns to keep out of potential physical and emotional harm by remaining still or moving away from the source of danger as directed by human instinct for survival. A young child has a natural urge to develop physical motor skills from birth in order to move away from danger, and to move towards an attachment figure for safety, *and* learning opportunities. In circumstances where an attachment figure is not available, the baby/child will learn to remain still within an adverse environment. This response has a detrimental effect upon learning and emotional wellbeing. If the environment has been deemed to be safe, then the child will use physical prowess to explore and learn from his or her proximal world.

A readiness to learn can be fulfilled as a child achieves a sense of the autobiographical self. The five stages of self were referred to in Chapter 1 in relation to gaps within adult learning due to a lack of appropriate stimulation in early childhood. The average child progresses through these five integral stages in the earliest years and achieves the autobiographical self at approximately five years of age (Trevarthan and Aitken, 2001).

- *Physical agent*– my physical world
- *Social agent*– my social world
- *Teleological agent*– understanding *and* applying knowledge of cause/effect
- *Intentional mental agent*– understanding my impact upon the world
- *Autobiographical self*– ready to learn

The skills which develop provide a blueprint for operating successfully in the world throughout childhood, adolescence, and early, middle, and latter stages of adulthood. Each person continues to increase his or her sense of self which is influenced by factors within the Ecological Systems of Human Development (Bronfenbrenner, 1979, 2005).

3. AN ACCESSIBLE SOURCE OF KNOWLEDGE

It is easy to place a child within a stimulating and vibrant learning environment, for example, a nursery or school setting. It is easy for a professional to initial an action point as completed in a child protection plan, or individual learning plan, through provision of a service; however the skill of being an effective educator depends on the practitioner's ability and capacity to seek out and to understand each child's interpretation of the world, and to support the child's motivation and desire to interact and to learn.

There is current debate in the United Kingdom on whether environments should be tailored for every child's potential needs or the child be supported to access generic learning opportunities. I believe that a combination of these two approaches represents inclusive pedagogy.

Active learning can be supported by educators who observe and record children's abilities rather than disabilities or inabilities, and who gain insight and comprehension from parents on the child's capacity to retain and apply knowledge. The most important input which a professional can offer to a child, in a context of learning within a service, is empowering the child to seek out knowledge, to nurture curiosity, and to promote secure attachment in order to increase involvement and emotional wellbeing. Children can be active agents in any environment.

4. EMOTIONAL LITERACY

Emotional literacy is a concept which enriches the existence of human beings who operate within a social world. It encompasses understanding of self, contributes to actualisation and executive functioning, and communication of need to attachment figures. Verbal communication of emotions may not be achievable or appropriate for every child. I feel that it is essential to promote emotional literacy for all children, and this means reviewing the current educational approach, and re-focusing upon the meaning rather than the projected outcome. Emotional literacy contributes to inclusion by supporting children to become active participants in their world of learning.

The promotion of emotional literacy in early years' services and primary schools has taken place in the United Kingdom over the past 20 years. If I ask practitioners to describe this concept, then invariably, the response will be the same, and it will focus upon an outcome. For example, a practitioner may comment that emotional literacy is "a child having the ability to talk about his or her emotions". If I seek further insight, the response might be, "a child understanding, *and* talking about his or her emotions" – two very different outcomes.

The promotion of emotional literacy commenced in the United Kingdom by focusing upon achievement of verbal emotional literacy. Comprehension of emotions also incorporates self-regulation. Bath (2017) promotes the importance of using verbal and non-verbal strategies in supporting children to communicate their emotions following trauma.

46 *Special needs to inclusion*

Emotional literacy for every child involves four steps. Children may require adult support to acquire and apply each step.

- Awareness of different emotions
- Ability to link actions, behaviour, and emotions
- Capacity to regulate action/behaviour and emotions
- Ability to understand social context of self-regulation

Example from practice

Three-year-old Najma has unusual behaviour in nursery. The health visitor has referred the little girl for specialist assessment; however, Najma is one of many children on the paediatric waiting list. A waiting list creates an opportunity for family learning intervention to commence as an interim measure, and I capitalise on the situation by raising this issue with the family. Najma attends the service on a daily basis accompanied by her mother Roshida, and paternal grandparents. The extended family stay in one household and support the children and each other collectively.

I have noticed that Najma demonstrates distinctive and recognisable patterns of behaviour. Her emotions are expressed dramatically to the world through her actions. It is common for children to acquire behavioural patterns as adults tend to react in the same predictable way each time; therefore, patterns provide a child with a sense of control by ensuring that he or she is prepared to absorb the adult's reaction.

Najma is unaware that she has different emotions. This little girl's feelings amalgamate into one episodic behavioural expression of her interpretation and reaction to her world. An outburst of anger and aggression by the three-year-old is modulated by physical exhaustion, and transcends into stress and despair. A practitioner will often intervene at this point. It may seem easier for an adult to react to a child who is crying as opposed to screaming.

Intervention by an adult can change an emotion. Najma's behaviour and actions escalate to hysteria, laughing and crying: ambivalent feelings as experienced by this child. An increase in physical contact from an adult can prompt a circular transition. Najma returns to a show of anger and aggression.

I explain this situation to the two generations of the family. The women lean forward towards me as if to gain reassurance. The meeting room is filled with anxiety which displays their need for a solution to this challenging, unfamiliar issue. The little girl's reactions are affecting the entire household: several generations discussing, and wondering, perplexed about Najma. I inadvertently mirror the actions of mother and mother-in-law. As I incline towards these service-users the dyad of professional and parent is primed to support learning. I read the signals of need, and I respond by seeking family expertise.

"Does Najma have a sensitive area to touch?" Gran talks rapidly to Roshida in Urdu, and points to Najma's inner wrist. Common tactile responding points are the inner wrists – individually or alternative pattern touching, behind a child's ears, bridge of the nose, nape of the neck, inner arms, soles of the feet, and tips of toes or fingers. I produce an adult facial make-up brush – perfect for little children – bristles are magically soft and cannot be pulled out by inquisitive teeth, the head is large and generous, a washable tool which can be spontaneously produced or easily hidden in a practitioner's pocket as required. I show the two generations of Najma's family how to stroke her wrist very gently with the brush. These actions should coincide with Najma demonstrating to us that her world is good – relaxed and happy body language.

Over time, children learn to link sensory stimulation with a specific emotion. The use of a locus, for example, a specific area to touch, equates with the early steps to emotional literacy. The advent of a nurturing tool during aggressive or distressed outbursts can support a nonverbal child to pause within this context. An induced pause provides the child with a momentary opportunity to reflect, and prompts a transition to a different emotional state. The child can be supported, over time, to de-escalate negative behaviours, actions, and emotions, and to undertake his or her transition into a positive mode. It is one approach to learning the first stage of emotional literacy and self-regulation for children who have complex needs.

What does this mean in theory and practice?

- A transitional period emerges between emotional states in which the child alters his or her emotional response.
- The child's capacity to alter emotional responses increases over time, and subsequently new patterns of behaviour are re-configured.
- The new patterns are based upon the child's regulation as opposed to repetitive emotional patterning.

5. SELF-REGULATION

There have been many changes in the rationale, and subsequent practical care and education of children, for example inclusion, attainment and standardised testing, personal interests, child centred and child led. This section focuses upon a feature of learners which is key to achievement within all

48 *Special needs to inclusion*

these contexts: self-regulation. Self-regulation is a necessary skill in order for human beings to operate effectively in a society which presents implicit, and explicit social rules within multiple contexts.

A child's perspective.

- **How do I relate to my world?**

    Babies are born with the instinct to seek out an attachment figure and to understand the world through the behaviour and reactions of a primary carer. New-born babies and young children are attracted to human faces, with a particular focus upon eyes. Eyes denote emotion and intent. Experience of initial relationships in life form a blueprint, a master-copy which the child remembers, and reproduces to support him or her in the creation of future relationships. Expectations are formed in the early stages of life, and comparisons are made from one relationship to another.

- **What do I need from my world?**

    This is a complex area of learning for a child. In order to know what he or she needs, a child has to interpret the physical and emotional signals within his or her own body. For example, feeling hungry, tired, or lonely. Subsequently a child has to determine how to ask for help and identify a reliable source. In order to achieve deep-level learning, a child has to be aware of current knowledge, and to be motivated to seek out further information and understanding.

- **How do I recognise my achievements?**

    It is important that children do not develop dependency on adults affirming their achievements. A child should be supported to identify a goal, which may be within a context limited by set choices, and to embrace the process to achieve this goal. The operational aspect may require the child to seek advice, practical input, and encouragement from adults or peers; however, personal recognition of achievement leads to an increase in self-esteem and emotional wellbeing. This approach is beginning to be utilised within education (Parker, Rose and Gilbert, 2016).

Example from practice

Six-year-old Kevin has attempted to draw an equilateral triangle as depicted by his teacher on the whiteboard. Kevin stares at the large blue shape which looks down upon the children from behind the teacher's desk, gives a cursory glance at his pencil representation, and raises his hand, "Is this right, Miss?"

It would be a quick response to say yes or no to the little boy. Yes would establish the child's dependency on adult recognition of achievement. No would induce negative emotions in Kevin. "What's the point!" is a familiar cry that I hear from school children. Negativity can overpower the motivation to learn and minimise capacity to seek out comprehension. Emotions can lead or obstruct intellectual development.

It is invaluable to spend a few minutes of time supporting Kevin to self-reflect, to make a personal assessment of his work, and to re-direct him to the processes associated with the expected outcome. Optimum teaching can be encapsulated in these few minutes promoting Kevin's development of his teleological self by comparing the teacher's instructions, his attempts, and the potential end product. An alternative comment from Kevin, "Miss, I think I did it!" demonstrates this young learner's foundation for personal recognition and attainment.

- **How do I cope with my adversities?**

    Practitioners can support children by observing each child's reactions, verbally tracking the child's movements, and affirming practical strategies which he or she accesses in response to adversity. An awareness of personal coping skills is an essential attribute throughout a lifespan.

Example from practice

I introduced an ice-breaker at the beginning of a presentation on resilience. A group of social workers were asked to identify personal strategies which were used to unwind at the end of a long working day.

As one of the participants collected the fluorescent Post-Its, and displayed them creatively in a big circle on the carpet, it quickly became obvious that there were many similarities in the results. Walking the dog, having a bath, Sudoku on the train, reading the newspaper, listening to music, and eating were recurrent features in this light-hearted exercise.

A more serious interpretation of the ice-breaker reveals that adults gain resilience by participating in physical and intellectual activities relative to their interests. The coping strategies which children apply can also be placed in these categories. From childhood to adulthood, it seems that the needs, and responses of human beings, change very little in the maintenance of good mental and physical health.

50 *Special needs to inclusion*

- **How do I achieve deep-level learning?**

   As mentioned previously, deep-level learning encompasses the use of sensory exploration, scaffolding from memory of previous experiences, and extrapolating, and using imagination to extend learning and to satisfy curiosity for knowledge.

Example from practice

Five-year-old Bobby observes his father hitting his mother on a regular basis. When Bobby entered our service, he remembered this influential role-modelling from home and hit the girls in nursery. The rationale for behaviour management strategies is self-regulation, and the team considered Bobby's needs. It seems that he had an immature sense of self. Promotion of the curriculum takes place in a context of children's interests; therefore it was decided by parent and key worker that Bobby's passion for noise and music would be utilised.

This young boy gained great satisfaction from banging a drum loudly, repetitively, and forcibly. Little children tend to bang a drum until exhausted as the intensive multi-sensory feedback stimulates the children to repeat the action in order to maintain the high-level stimulus. Over time Bobby was supported to start, to stop, to drum loudly, to drum quietly, to use one stick or two sticks, to drum while sitting, to drum while marching or walking, to drum on tip-toe, to drum while standing on one leg – endless possibilities were suggested by parent and key worker embracing this developmental stage for Bobby.

The context was fulfilled, and Bobby gained an understanding of his physical and teleological self. Regulating his physical action of hitting female peers became easier for Bobby as time progressed, and he slowly gained an understanding of how to relate to his world, what he needed from his world, how to recognise his achievements, how to cope with adversities, and how to achieve deep-level learning within this protective environment. Bobby's inner working model changed. Initially the change was almost imperceptible, but gradually self-regulation supported a change in his interpretation, perceptions, behaviour, and emotions. A child's emotions should be understood and responded to in this context.

Included in the world of learning

The next section describes research and evolvement of practice based upon therapeutic pedagogy which has been used to support children within the context of early years' settings. I was involved in this process as a facilitator and participant before, during, and after the research project.

Ten years ago, in Glasgow, services were receiving large numbers of referrals for families in which the parents had long-term addictions: hard drugs, prescription drugs, alcohol, illegal highs, and combinations of these substances. It was assessed that parents were well-supported by a wide-range of professionals, for example, addiction workers, community re-integration team, housing, employment preparation, health, and education. It was noted that the children, particularly in the early years, were not fully engaged with learning environments; therefore, levels of involvement and wellbeing were low. An intervention was introduced, and researched, to facilitate the achievement of potential for these young children who were experiencing life in a context of adversities (Baldry and Moscardini, 2010).

Interventions do not support change per se, but provide opportunities for families to learn and to develop within a protective environment, supported by a skilled facilitator. The objective of intervention is changing the inner working model, the operational capacity, and executive functioning of the individuals and also the group, in a context of a family unit. Interventions are short-term measures in a context of funding and implementation. A future area of research, and development of practice, is the transitional period in which *newly acquired knowledge and understanding* are transferred into daily environments which are subject to a multitude of influences – predictable or otherwise.

The following is an account of pertinent aspects of one innovative approach to supporting vulnerable children to understand the sense of self, to gain resilience, to increase involvement and wellbeing, and to be included in the world of learning.

Butterflies

Early years' practitioners will recognise this term *butterflies* as applied to some of the children in their care. Workers will often describe the "butterfly effect" in nurseries as children who flit from activity to activity. Children who cannot settle at a play area. Children who cannot concentrate. Children who are excluded from learning. In reality, these children do have the capacity to achieve deep-level learning, but their concentration is easily disturbed by internal or external influences; therefore, interactions take place at the basic sensory level.

Internal factors relate to short or long-term trauma. For example, a child may appear vigilant as his inner working model has been programmed to maintain safety rather than explore learning opportunities. External factors are environmental. These influences may be local, for example, the interference from another child playing in the same area or familiar/unfamiliar noises from traffic, doors opening and closing, a phone ringing, a flock of seagulls, the clapping of helicopter blades, and workmen digging the roads. A child who is disturbed during learning requires a mature sense of self in order to return to the same activity, and to resume the same interactions at the same level of knowledge and understanding. If the autobiographical self is immature, then the child will move to another area and commence exploration at a sensory level.

Children may use strategies to support their needs either spontaneously or by reflecting upon the environmental aspects of the learning environment. One focus of nursery playrooms, and the early years of school, is to encourage cooperative play by children. It is essential that children are given opportunities to develop their play as appropriate to their *stages* of development rather than the norm associated with a child's *age* (Whitters, 2017).

Example from practice

*The stages of play are solitary, parallel, intermittent interaction, and cooperative. Nurseries and schools are set up to encourage children to progress through these social and intellectual stages of learning: tables with single chairs can face towards a wall or mirror in order to provide opportunities for **solitary play** and to minimise distractions, chairs side by side at a table promote **parallel play** – a child learns to tolerate the invasion of his play space by a peer, chairs facing at a small table with a centred activity can result in **intermittent interactions** between two children who seek the same stimulus, and finally grouped chairs facilitate **cooperative play** at a mature stage of the autobiographical self.*

Leuven Involvement/Wellbeing Scales

Ferre Laevers (1994) developed the Leuven Involvement and Wellbeing Scale as a guide to assessing a child's reaction to his world. These scales are very useful to promote understanding of learning processes, and to guide practitioners through the developmental patterns of children. The knowledge and understanding which is gained from reflection upon a child's level of achievement can be applied to the creation, and the updating of an individual learning plan. The focus should not be upon leading the child through each level of involvement, but provision of support in the form of an attachment figure, and an environment in which the child can consolidate his or her learning at one level, in addition to the availability of new opportunities. This may incur repetitive play over time. Repetition is necessary to create patterns of interaction, and to inform the inner working model. Consolidation of skills supports an increase in emotional wellbeing which will directly motivate the child to seek out further opportunities, and venture towards a deeper level of investigation and interaction. The child's increase in wellbeing will be partnered with an increase in the level of involvement.

The following aspects relate to interpretation of the five stages from the Leuven Scale (Laevers, 1994) within a practice context of early years (Whitters, 2017).

Child involvement

1 *The child may observe the environment without involvement or create a barrier between himself and the setting, for example by covering his or her eyes or turning towards the carer.*
2 *The child's involvement at a basic sensory level is easily interrupted by an external factor which stops his interaction. The child may subsequently transfer his attention to a different activity, and commence interaction at the same basic sensory level.*
3 *The child's involvement does not have a focus. He is easily distracted by internal or external influences, but can resume interaction with the same activity at a sensory level.*
4 *The child appears to have a plan and focus for involvement in play. He is able to concentrate on the activity for short periods by filtering out potential distractions.*
5 *Fully engaged in meaningful play – the child demonstrates that he is following his interests, creating, and implementing a plan, and responding to his needs by accessing support as required. The child demonstrates a deep level of learning through the use of three stages – sensory exploration, implementation of knowledge and understanding from implicit or explicit memories, and extrapolating by using his imagination, and quest for knowledge.*

Child wellbeing

1 *The child shows clear signals of distress and may attempt to leave the environment or to seek support from the carer. The child demonstrates rejection of the learning opportunities by his physical and emotional responses.*
2 *The child may observe but not interact with the environment. Facial expression and neutral posture show little or no emotion, and he will keep his body still.*
3 *Facial expression and posture demonstrate that the child is beginning to relax and feels comfortable to interact within the environment. The child may stand and play in one area.*

4   The child demonstrates obvious signs of self-confidence and enjoyment in play. His increasing sense of self will be demonstrated by an increase in physical movement throughout the learning environment.
5   The child demonstrates obvious signs of self-confidence and high self-esteem. His body language expresses a high level of wellbeing by the use of physical skills to increase interaction with the environment.

Increasing involvement and wellbeing

The aim of the original intervention programme was to provide children, who were growing up in adverse socio-economic circumstances, with an opportunity to understand experiences and emotions, develop self-control and responsibility, and ultimately build resilience and achieve potential. Practitioners, and several parents were trained in the *Child-Parent-Relationship Training* by Bratton, Landreth, Kellam, and Blackard (2006), which incorporates client-centred principles from play therapy.

A series of individual sessions with specific conceptual toys gave each child aged two to five years the opportunity to develop a secure attachment with a facilitator or parent within an environment conducive to exploration, mastery, consolidation, and extension of skills. The conceptual toys support emotional expression. This half hour intervention occurred once a week with a child and trained facilitator.

Many children who have low emotional wellbeing do not use direct or prolonged eye contact with adults or peers. The vulnerable child has learned that his attachment cues have not been responded to in a consistent manner; therefore he or she refrains from the use of eye contact to communicate his or her needs, wants, and ambitions. Artefacts can be offered in response to this need, in any play session, whether a formal intervention or throughout daily experiences. Useful objects are toy binoculars, goggles, sun glasses, mobile phones, cameras, cardboard tubes, and thin transparent silk scarves. The common feature is the child gaining control of when and how he or she makes eye contact. I feel that these artefacts can be regarded as enablers to communication. Some researchers may describe their use as creating a barrier between the child and his or her world. Toy mobile phones are particularly popular with children as a familiar tool used frequently by primary carers. The use of a phone supports a child to activate his or her verbal skills, and the subsequent increase in self-confidence can result in accompanying eye contact.

Behaviour management was encompassed within the promotion of social, emotional, and environmental boundaries, which enabled the child to learn what he or she can and cannot do, to re-direct negative behaviour appropriately, to recognise different emotions, and to link descriptive words to actions and behaviour. Astramovich (1999) commented that child-centred play with definable limits supports a child to establish self-control.

There were three distinct steps to supporting the child to self-regulate his or her emotions and behaviour.

- *Acknowledge* child's emotions and actions – simple clear phrases.

  For example, I know that you want to cut the doll's hair.

- *Communicate* the social boundary – not a reprimand, just a statement of fact, a learning opportunity.

  For example, the doll's hair is not for cutting.

- *Target* an alternative action for the child which is relevant to the context – teach the child social behaviours; adults incorrectly assume that children can work out the acceptable behaviours in each setting.

  For example, cut the paper instead.

Children's behaviour

Behaviour is a child's language:

- A communication strategy which represents a child's interpretation, and comprehension of his or her world through actions and behaviour.

  Actions are regarded as "what a child does".
  Behaviour describes "how he or she does it".
  Emotions represent "how he or she feels".

- A communication strategy to actively demonstrate emotion.
- A communication strategy which inadvertently demonstrates emotion.

Managing a child's behaviour, as opposed to a child's self-regulation of behaviour, is an adult reaction to a negative social outcome. Workers will often be given recognition of this perceived achievement by colleagues or parents; however, adult management of children's behaviour, regulation of the actions of our youngest service-users, and the subsequent restriction upon learning, are not outcomes which are relevant to 21st century pedagogies.

Positive social outcomes are necessary and desirable; therefore, during consideration of policy and practice responses, it is important to investigate the concept of behaviour, and to explore the component parts in a context of self-regulation, attainment, and inclusion.

Over the years, practitioners have been taught, and applied various approaches to behaviour management within early years' settings as applicable to trends and policies. The practical implementation changed, but the principles were always the same – highlight the negative behaviour and administer consequences. Through reflection, it seems that learning was minimal and focused upon the child recognising and responding to the power of an adult. The child's self-esteem was affected, and there were an impact upon the attachment relationship and an increasing dependency upon adult instruction.

Behaviour and transitions

As mentioned previously, adults often assume that children can work out the appropriate social behaviours if the negative behaviour is criticised. Adults have a lifetime of experience, and it is essential to share comprehension with children. Explicit social rules can appear indefinable to children, and implicit social rules are sometimes imperceptible.

Children who have autistic spectrum disorder will be particularly challenged by social interactions. Autistic spectrum disorder can result in difficulty with transitions. Every setting and home environment has multiple transitions. Parents and professionals identify techniques and strategies to support transitions – a parent's expertise is invaluable in this area of work. Photograph prompts can provide a child with information on expected changes and support a child to re-focus by promoting knowledge and understanding of change.

Some children may not have the ability to interpret this information from a photograph, or the capacity to focus upon the laminated picture which has interrupted their play; however transitions invariably incur physical movement, and if a child can be supported to accept physical change, then it can support intellectual and emotional acceptance, and re-focussing.

Example from practice

Four-year-old Jayne has a diagnosis of autistic spectrum disorder. She demonstrates solitary play. It can appear that Jayne does not notice her peers as she pushes another child aside at the sand-tray or climbs over a boy who lies on the floor playing with the trains. Observation presents understanding of these actions to practitioners and parent, and it is obvious that Jayne interprets the other children as obstructions in her pathways to learning.

Jayne actively avoids eye contact with adults or peers. This behaviour is not a result of negative responses, but the little girl's inner working model does not support a need for social interaction. Jayne has not yet connected intellectual development with relationships.

The result is that Jayne cannot copy her peers or adults. Learning from role-modelling is one of the richest sources for intellectual, physical, and emotional development. Learning through personal solitary interactions with the world takes time, and requires repeated exposure to many different experiences. Jayne's current focus is learning about her world from a personal perspective.

As Jayne enters the playroom, she runs to her chosen table, and staff make sure that this reference point remains consistently in the same place at drop-off time. Jayne can be supported to learn by hand-over-hand teaching. She has independently explored large chunky beads and laces on several occasions, at a sensory level. Gentle hand-over-hand support by a responsive practitioner enabled Jayne to understand the task, to identify the location of centred holes in each bead, to feel the stiff end of each lace, to thread, to seek, to anticipate and to recover the lace as it came through the dark hole in the bead, to experience the thrill of achievement, to repeat, to consolidate, to master!

One activity can be used for multiple learning opportunities if a child demonstrates an interest in the subject matter. Jayne has returned to this activity each day, she has a goal, she recognises personal achievement, she extends her skills, and she understands speed within a task. Colours, matching, sorting, and counting are waiting to be accessed on the learning horizon . . . . Jayne's laughter represents her prowess.

Snack time – Jayne is immersed in bead-play. Her mother demonstrates tension as she anticipates her daughter's resistance. A myriad of emotions can be read from the mother's facial expression and body language. Physical movement is required for this transition, so I gently move Jayne back and forward as she explores the wooden necklace. At first Jayne is unaware that I am becoming involved in her world, then her body starts to move from side to side, she continues to focus upon the beads. I stand Jayne upon her feet, she clings tightly to the necklace, and I continue to move her gently – side to side – informing her inner being that physical movement is the next stage. Jayne allows me to support her to move from floor play to the snack table, her body sways back and forward – the physical transition is taking place.

A quick-thinking staff slides Jayne's plate of fruit into eye contact, on the table. Jayne's comprehension is complete, necklace is dropped, and I sit her onto a little red chair. Jayne is re-focused – a smooth transition encompasses learning as appropriate to stage of need rather than age. Jayne's mother looks tearful, and comments from the side-lines, "Thank you."

When transitions are seamless, then social rules cannot always be identified by children. There may be little realisation that the child has moved from one area to another, and it is important that expectations of behaviour are communicated effectively to each child. Negative behaviour often results from a child's lack of knowledge and understanding of the social context.

What does this mean in theory and practice?

- Jayne's inner working model is being re-configured.
- Physical skill leads intellectual capacity – an increase in knowledge and understanding.
- Neural transmissions seek connections in the brain, and repetitive actions strengthen the information processing system of this young learner.
- Jayne's mother, the primary attachment figure, is acquiring knowledge of skills in supporting her daughter to operate effectively within different microsystems.
- Jayne's mother is an active agent in the professional–parent partnership of family learning.

The inclusion agenda is politically based and can appear to be far removed from activities within services. Inclusive pedagogy has regenerated and rejuvenated the implementation of services to all families in the child's earliest years. The next chapter reviews the impact of innovative practice upon policy.

References

Abajobir, A. A. (2017). Childhood maltreatment and adulthood poor sleep quality: A longitudinal study. *Internal Medicine Journal*. Retrieved 10 September 2017, from http://onlinelibrary.wiley.com/doi/10.1111/imj.13459/

Astramovich, R. L. (1999). *Play therapy theories: A comparison of three approaches*. Retrieved 1 May 2017, from www.http://ericfac.piccard.csc.com

Baldry, H., and Moscardini, L. (2010). *Letting the children lead*. Retrieved 9 July 2017, from www.therobertsontrust.org.uk

Bath, H. (2017). The trouble with trauma. *Scottish Journal of Residential Care, volume 16, number 1*. Retrieved 10 September 2017, from www.celcis.org/knowledge.bank/search.bank/journal/Scottish-journal-residential-child-care-vol-16

Bergen, D., and Woodin, M. (2017). *Brain research and childhood education, implications for educators, parents and society*. Abingdon: Routledge.

Bomber, L. M. (2007). *Inside I am hurting, practical strategies for supporting children with attachment difficulties in schools*. London: Worth Publishing Ltd.

Bomber, L. M. (2011). *What about me? – Inclusive strategies to support pupils with attachment difficulties make it through the school day*. London: Worth Publishing Ltd.

Bratton, S. C., Landreth, G. L., Kellam, T., and Blackard, S. R. (2006). *Child/parent participation therapy treatment manual*. New York: Routledge.

Bronfenbrenner, U. (1979). *The ecology of human development* (2nd edition). Cambridge, MA: Harvard University Press.

Bronfenbrenner, U. (2005). *Making human beings human*. Thousand Oaks, CA: Sage.

Bronfenbrenner, U., and Morris, P. A. (2006). The bioecological model of human development. In W. Damon and R. M. Lerner (Eds.), *Handbook of child psychology* (volume 1, pp. 796–798, 800, 810–815). Hoboken, NJ: Wiley & Sons.

Cabral, J. (2014). *How Solihull approach can fit with Scotland's parenting initiatives*. Edinburgh: Scottish Government.

Centre on the Developing Child. (2016). *From best practice to breakthrough impacts*. Harvard: National Scientific Council on the Developing Child.

Cozolino, L. (2013). *The social neuroscience of education: Optimising attachment and learning in the classroom*. London: Norton & Company.

Department for Children and Schools. (1996). *The education act (1996)*. London: Department for Children and Schools.

Department for Children and Schools. (2001). *Special educational needs and disability act (2001)*. London: Department for Children and Schools.

Department for Children and Schools. (2014). *Children and families act (2014)*. London: Department for Children and Schools.

Laevers, F. (1994). *Defining and assessing quality in early childhood education* (Studia Pedagogica). Belgium: Leuven University Press.

Mazzucchelli, T. G., and Sanders, M. (2010). Facilitating practitioner flexibility within an empirically supported intervention: Lessons from a system of parenting support. *Clinical Psychology Science and Practice*. Retrieved 30 September 2016, from http://journals.sagepub.com/doi/pdf/10.1177/1524838016658876

McCrory, E. J., Gerin, M. I., and Viding, E. (2017). Annual research review: Childhood maltreatment, latent vulnerability and the shift to preventative psychiatry – The contribution of functional brain imaging. *Journal of Child Psychology and Psychiatry, volume 58, number 4*. Retrieved 3 April 2017, from http://onlinelibrary.wiley.com/doi/10.1111/jcpp.12713/full

Moran, P., Ghate, D., and van der Merwe, A. (2004). *What works in parenting support? A review of the international evidence* (pp. 49, 57, 63, 68, 75, 80, 85, 93–99, 104–108, 112, 122–132). London: Department for Education and Skills.

Nursery World. (2016). *Evidenced-based parenting programmes*. Retrieved 30 May 2016, from www.nurseryworld.co.uk/nursery-world/news/1158168/programmes-that-boost-childrens-development-rated

Parker, R., Rose, J., and Gilbert, L. (2016). *Attachment aware schools: An alternative to behaviourism in supporting children's behaviour*. Retrieved 16 September 2017, from www.cypsomersethealth.org/resources/SECP/attachment-aware-schools.docx

Rogers, C. (1990). *The Carl Rogers reader* (pp. 64–65, 75, 108, 116–118, 135–137, 221–227, 251–252, 271–272). Cornwall: MPG Books Ltd.

Rutter, M. (2012). *Annual research review resilience – Clinical implications.* Retrieved 16 September 2017, from http://onlinelibrary.wiley.com/doi/10.1111/j.1469-7610-2012.02615.x/abstract

Sanders, M. R. (2008). Triple P-positive parenting programme as a public health approach to strengthening parenting. *Journal of Family Psychology, volume 22, number 3.* New Jersey: American Psychological Association.

Scottish Executive. (2004). *The education (additional support for learning) (Scotland) act 2004.* Edinburgh: Scottish Executive.

Scottish Government. (2008). *A guide to getting it right for every child.* Edinburgh: Scottish Government.

Scottish Government. (2009). *The education (additional support for learning) (Scotland) act 2009.* Edinburgh: Scottish Government.

Scottish Government. (2016). *The (education) Scotland act 2016.* Edinburgh: Scottish Government.

Solihull Approach Parenting Group Research. (2009). Solihull approach parenting group research and nice guidelines. Retrieved 20 March 2009, from https://solihullapproachparenting.com/quick-guide-to-the-solihull-approach/

Trevarthan, C., and Aitken, K. J. (2001). Infant intersubjectivity: Research, theory, and clinical applications. *Journal of Child Psychology and Psychiatry, volume 42.* Cambridge: Cambridge University Press.

United Nations Educational, Scientific and Cultural Organisation (UNESCO). (1994). *The Salamanca statement and framework for action on special needs education.* Paris: UNESCO.

Van der Kolk, B. (2003). *The neurobiology of childhood trauma and abuse.* Retrieved 17 May 2016, from www.researchgate.net/publication/10779024

Whitters, H. G. (2017). *Nursery nurse to early years' practitioner: Role, relationships and responsibilities.* Abingdon: Routledge.

3 Leading the workforce
Practice to policy

Practice to policy

There are many different formal and informal routes to practice influencing policy. Governments seek out evidence from practitioners within public consultations during the early stages of policy development. Ministers will also visit a range of settings to observe examples of good practice in the field. Traditionally, information is gathered through the formality of inspections. Early years' services may be subject to regular inspection by different bodies who represent the authority which upholds the right of children to receive appropriate care and education. Examples are Care Inspectorate, Her Majesty's Inspectorate of Education (HMIE), local council, and funding bodies. Informal feedback on service delivery from parents and children is retrieved within inspections, formally recorded, and contributes to grading the value of a service in a national context for public access. This feedback encompasses parent and children's views on family learning, inclusion, and attainment. Additionally, information may be used as a contribution to triangulation of data, and it may also contribute to validity within research and evaluation studies. Qualitative and quantitative methods are used to gain comprehension of each organisation's delivery of services, and to promote choices to service-users.

Inclusion and attainment

Principles of inclusion can be implemented with validity by using a variety of approaches. Models in the United Kingdom reflect similar principles: the Scottish Curriculum for Excellence promotes a flexible approach to learning for all children, and the English practice model encompasses influences from elements of mainstream topics and individual development (Hobbs, 2009). Curricula are traditionally constructed in relation to developmental levels, and ages and stages of the average child in accordance with professionally determined norms of achievement; therefore attainment is recorded in a context of age-related educational output.

A dichotomy between recording statistics in a context of curricular outcomes, and achievement of children with severe and profound needs, was highlighted in research by South Lanarkshire council in Scotland (Rees, Tully, and Ferguson, 2017). This council published a guidance framework, for children with additional support needs, to be implemented in parallel with Curriculum for Excellence which is applicable to all Scottish children aged 3–18 years (Scottish Executive, 2004).

Rees et al. (2017) describe an absence of observable norms which precludes grouping children who have additional support needs in order to record generic statistics. The authors indicate that there is a lack of national evidence which publicises the value of current curricular approaches in the United Kingdom. Bergen and Woodin (2017) researched the same issues from an international perspective and commented that there is insufficient evidence to identify the optimum educational environment for children with additional support for learning needs; however inclusion within a mainstream setting is an increasing response throughout the world to optimise education of all children.

There remains a question of clarity in the processes to recording attainment of curricular outcomes in a context of inclusion. For example, statistics in relation to attainment of national standards of mathematics and literacy outcomes may be based upon a whole school population and not give statistical recognition to individual attainment in the executive functioning of children with additional support needs.

Care and education are currently delivered within a context of change as inclusive education is put into practice within services. The early years' workforce is learning "on the job" and implementing legislation progressively by responding to the needs of each child. Professional expertise in the creation of policy, guidance, and implementation will continue to increase over time, but there is already an invaluable resource available which can remain untapped by organisations: families.

Prior to attending services, parents accumulate expertise which is focused upon knowledge and understanding of their child. It is often the case that parents do not have realisation of the depth and relevance of their comprehension until it is sought by professionals. The act of seeking knowledge from families in order to influence professional practice raises the personal and public status of families. Extended family members are an additional rich source for information which can contribute deep insight into the child's learning needs, influences, and identification of potential protective factors within a range of circumstances. Family learning is relevant to inclusion, and this approach to educating and caring for children is already transforming services and is a prominent aspect of future national planning in the United Kingdom (Schrader-McMillan and Barlow, 2017; Scottish Government, 2017).

Example from practice

> *The autumn gales have commenced, and the children enter our family service with dripping jackets and muddy wellingtons. Emmanuel is four years old, and he has been diagnosed with autistic spectrum disorder (ASD). His mother Owala had previously informed me that her three boys were "on the spectrum." Owala's mood seems low this Friday afternoon. Every practitioner knows that Fridays and Mondays are difficult periods for vulnerable families. Friday is spent in trepidation of potential adversities over the weekend, and Monday is a day of recovery from physical and emotional influences within the family environment.*
>
> *As Owala sits Emmanuel on the cloakroom floor to put on his favourite Postman Pat slippers, I slide along the bench to observe her wellbeing as we chat about the weather! I seek insight into Owala's emotions and prompt an honest response by presenting two options. Options normalise help-seeking for families.*
>
> *"Owala, you seem quiet today. Is everything okay **or** are you having one of these tricky Fridays?"*
>
> *This mother sits her son on the bench beside me, he swings his legs to play hide and seek with the Postman Pat slippers, and I place my arm around his shoulders. Owala is concerned that Emmanuel is bumping into furniture and often has bruises on his face. I inform her that I had observed Emmanuel running in the nursery garden yesterday. The rectangular grass represents an inner-city nursery eco-space, surrounded by multi-coloured metal fencing – carefully spaced to avoid exit by an inquisitive child but allowing a view of the vehicles which slow down as they approach the steep hill. I had noticed that little Emmanuel ran quickly towards the fencing, and he did not reduce pace as he approached the man-made boundary. Emmanuel had bumped against the fence-posts, and he looked surprised that his hidden plan had been thwarted.*
>
> *Owala interrupted me, and tapped my arm as she smiled and eagerly contributed to the discussion, "I know why that happened. Emmanuel does it in the park. He is looking between the spaces of the fencing, and does not notice the metal posts." We exchanged a look which represented our shared understanding of this little boy's interpretation of his world. Parental and professional expertise merges. Family learning in practice . . . .*

We discuss a potential solution for the nursery garden – cardboard tied along the fencing for the children to create chalk marks, and to give Emmanuel affirmation of the environmental boundary. An increased awareness of this child's learning needs has been established. Seek help, give help, help others, and help yourself – it is a well-trodden pathway which can support development and comprehension of self. Family learning can potentially occur in many contexts, informal and spontaneous, to formal, meticulously planned, and implemented. Family learning can occur within many time-frames, minutes, or months. Family learning can use many media, but the universal feature is a therapeutic alliance between service-provider and service-user.

The rationale of family learning is based upon upskilling, empowering, and equipping families to understand themselves as individuals, and within a family unit, in order to develop transferrable skills which can be applied within a range of circumstances. Family learning principles promote professionals as educators, and families as developing persons, but roles are inter-changeable, and expertise crosses the boundary of service-provider and service-user. Family input can provide a reliable, valuable source of knowledge and understanding of a child to an integrated team of multi-disciplinary professionals.

Organisational memory, pedagogy, and practice

Organisational memory is applicable to every workplace, and the concept is associated with sustaining and building upon good practice over time, despite changes in personnel. In 2001, one writer described a modern approach to management as the use of perception and facilitation which led to a self-sustaining company (Henry, 2001). During the intervening years, these features have been recognised as actions which contribute to organisational memory.

- *Organisational memory* encompasses core principles, values, and beliefs of a service which may be publicised in the format of a mission statement.
- *Pedagogy* refers to the organisation's approach to delivery and implementation of services to the service-users – organisational culture.
- *Practice* reflects, and promotes local policy, and national guidance within interactions between service-provider and service-user.

Practice, in a context of relationship-based services, incurs the use of personality from each worker. Personality affects our actions, behaviour, and emotions. Over time, each employee contributes to and shapes an organisation by influencing practice, pedagogy, and organisational memory.

Personnel in a workplace are the collators, retainers, and disseminators of the information which gives an identity to an organisation and publicises worthiness of service. Personnel are the implementation tools to activate an organisational culture. Personnel are the safe-guarders of pedagogy. Personnel are responsible and accountable individually, locally, and nationally. Personnel are key to sustaining and developing organisational memory.

What does this mean in theory and practice?

The Social-Address Model (Magnusson and Stattin, 2006) is a theoretical system which acknowledges the unique reaction of each human being to his or her environment. The workplace environment functions and changes as a continuously ongoing process of interaction and interdependence of employees as individuals, and collectively as a group. The process demonstrates that each human being is an active part of a complex dynamic person–environment system relating to the world of employment. The working environment supports the total functioning and development of the individual, and the social unit.

The ability of an employee to recognise operational patterns, and to transfer knowledge into practice, can lead to an environment in which each worker is an active intentional force. This status relates to the autobiographical sense of self as an *intentional mental agent.*

Intellectual curiosity is a catalyst for the occurrence of this process which encompasses a desire and motivation to learn through seeking an increase in understanding, and subsequently developing the application of skills. Additionally, this attribute invokes an awareness in an employee that learning is continuous, and accumulative throughout a career. I believe that professionals gain expertise in a field of work, but there is not a definitive status of "being an expert." Expertise encompasses intellectual curiosity, and a realisation that additional knowledge, deeper insight, and an increase in comprehension can be sought and gained within a fluid ongoing process.

The Social-Address Model supports an understanding of the complexities of the workforce, and the impact of organisational memory upon the operational capacity of each service. A workforce is a composite entity: individuals of different ages and stages in their careers who are motivated by vocation or finance, individuals who form cliques, individuals who form teams, or individuals who practice alone but strive to identify with, and to represent a hidden extended workforce. Gaining knowledge of policies and procedures is an integral first task in a work role, and this act is encompassed within every induction of new staff. The first view that the workforce have of a new member of the team is an individual, with head bowed over an enormous paper folder, reading avidly to demonstrate competence on induction day.

The paper documents represent years of development and progress of an organisation which have been formatted into strap-lines. Policies are often generically worded, cut and paste from neighbouring organisations, change the header, add a footer, show willingness to conform and to meet standards. Policies and procedures are necessary and provide a framework for practice within an organisation which is bound further by national standards, and beyond by international regulations, and ultimately by formal expectations from nations who are united in their beliefs.

Allocation of financial autonomy to each organisation is a current approach to competent use of funding, and responsive care to local needs. An additional outcome is diverting accountability from a main funder such as a local authority to each service. This feature of 21st century strategic planning has prompted organisations to focus upon operational potential in the form of workforce personnel. The foundation of organisational memory is formed by policies, but these paper mandates are transformed by personnel activating standards through daily interactions with service-users, and other service-providers.

Childcare and education is a profession which attracts long-term workers, and *good practice* in an organisation often becomes synonymous with personnel. Work roles are described in terms of named employees, for example, "Asma's job", "Mark's role", "Peter's interventions", and "Mary's way of working". I notice new-starts are often implicitly, and perhaps unintentionally, challenged by this interpretation of roles, for example, the comment "How are you managing Peter's job?" may be construed as an innocent social gambit or a passage of rite into the culture of a team.

Workers gain recognition by implicit or explicit association with good practice which is amalgamated to a job role. This status is a necessary contribution to support employees' sustainability and longevity within a workforce, and encourages commitment, and loyalty to an organisation; however, what about staff turnover? What about the new-start who is keen to embrace *a role,* but not replicate *Peter's role?*

Transitions in the workplace

Staff changes should be regarded as formal transition periods. This approach leads to reflection and identification of good organisational practice as opposed to personality of an individual. Transition presents opportunities to revisit principles and values, and to clarify expectations of practice which relate directly to the organisation. The exercise serves to minimise the effect from personal traits which can become entrenched within a role, and exposes any deviation from core aspects if a role has been implemented by the same employee over time.

Teams encounter turbulent periods in which relationships and delivery of service can be affected by the characteristics of individual workers: overpowering strength or weakness in communication skills, leadership potential or ill-founded desire to lead, inexperience or restricted experiences, external support or external distraction, good health or ill-health of the employee. Gaps can be filled by the skills of new personnel, and these may be latent. Daily working environments present challenges which release hidden talents from new-starts, and re-configure organisational memory.

The marriage of organisational memory and pedagogy is potentially informed by findings from research, changes to practice, innovation from new-starts, and cooperation or strife in the workplace microsystems. Organisational memory influences pedagogy, and enriches practice within the community context by supporting implementation of services in accordance with cultural sensitivity. Relationships between professionals need to be considered and nurtured in the same way as the professional–parent relationships. It is easy to criticise teams, and individuals, and to promote optimum outcomes as the only recognisable goal for services. It can appear that policy demands, and expects effective integrated working to occur consistently within service delivery. Any relationship-based work should recognise the vulnerabilities and learning needs of each adult whether professionals or parents. Relationships evolve over time, peaks and troughs of positivity and negativity which should be observed and responded to, and ultimately absorbed into the minutiae of daily working life.

Example from practice

A line manager and two senior staff gather the trappings to support a challenging meeting: A4 paper as opposed to Post-It notes, pens and pencils, calculator, job descriptions, laptop, and steaming mugs of coffee. An early years' practitioner is leaving the organisation. The team agree upon the old adage in every workplace "nobody is indispensable!"

However, roles and responsibilities become immersed within the personality of a long-term employee, and influenced by his or her personal and professional perceptions, and interpretation of practice. Active implementation of duties can appear to represent the job description for a post. Tacitly each member of this senior team is considering "can the irreplaceable employee be replaced?"

The line manager induces a positive attitude into the initial stages of the meeting as staff pull up chairs to the table, and resign themselves to an hour of negotiation. She acknowledges the difficulty in filling a vacancy which cannot be advertised immediately. The practical reality of financial constraints is an unwelcome addition to the conversation. She listens and accepts the concerns as voiced by two senior staff who feel vulnerable as a gap in service is envisaged, and she takes time to consider the needs of the organisation.

Returning to core values is a significant aspect of managing these employment circumstances, and creating a plan which focuses upon the future rather than attempting to recreate the past. The line manager leads this senior team through a discussion, revisiting the mission statement, identifying needs of service-users, objectively perusing the original job description, and revising and clarifying appropriate changes. Two A4 pages later and the team disperse with the semblance of a plan which was constructed through awareness of organisational memory, and pedagogy. Transitions between employees always incur changes, and can reflect good practice by capitalising upon opportunities to develop a service.

What does this mean in theory and practice?

- The workplace is composed of multiple entities – personnel. Personnel operate as individuals or form groups, for example teams.
- Personnel operate within microsystems in the context of teams. The teams may function independently and/or collectively within the organisation.
- Organisational memory reflects the core principles, values, and beliefs on which the organisation is founded despite changes in personnel.
- Organisational memory underpins the creation of mesosystems which link workplace teams, contribute to effective communication, and consistency of practice output.
- Intellectual curiosity provides a motivational force for change and development in workplaces.

Constructive criticism/learning and development

Each human being operates from a distinctive and unique inner working model. Interpretation of the world of work is dependent on internal and external influences upon the employee, which is based on his or her past and current experiences, and expectations. Memories of significant events can be explicit or implicit as described by the research of Robinson and Brown (2016). These authors identified that biological reactions affect the sensory processing of an event which may result in explicit memories being triggered by environmental features. Alternatively, implicit memories are fragmented and linked to emotional reactions. These features affect the operational capacity of each employee.

It is easy to criticise your own practice as most workplaces actively highlight actions which do not meet the requirements of the organisation or the line manager. These highlighted actions are usually composites of *good enough* practice and *areas for development.* Supporting and nurturing the development of employees should always be based upon a culture of learning.

Constructive criticism is often used as verbal packaging to justify the delivery of negative feedback on practice to employees. Every employee brings rich and varied experiences into the workplace. In times of emotional stress, pedagogy of previous employment may come to the fore. The cry of "but that's how we were taught in my last workplace," is a common response to criticism. A lack of knowledge and understanding usually surfaces from an investigation of *poor practice*, and subsequently joint accountability for worker and line manager.

It is essential that line managers seek out comprehension of context during support and supervision sessions with employees which focus upon negative and positive examples of practice. Learning should be gained from an exploration of strategic and operational processes, in addition to achievement or failure to achieve an identified outcome. Processes are often indicated in a coloured flow-chart of organisational practice; however, in any work with families which centres on an increase in responsibility and independent decision-making, contextual influences can create deviations from the norm.

Reciprocal exchanges in a context of learning and development bring deeper understanding to personnel *and* to line managers. The promotion of self-awareness, self-critique, and self-reflection should be encompassed within organisational memory, influence pedagogy, and be demonstrated in the implementation of service.

Example from practice

It was approaching the end of another working day in our service. Five minutes to five. I was waiting for the laptop to complete updates so that I could close the lid on another session, and I became aware of interactions between practitioners.

One practitioner commented to her colleague about a family, newly-referred to the service, "I just don't know what to do . . . ." The theory would tell us that this is a direct signalling of need within the microsystem of a workplace. Practice indicates this is a cry for help, one practitioner to another. It would be easy to respond quickly and dismiss this signal – after all, it is five minutes before home-time; however, it is essential that practitioners support one another by interpreting these comments in the context of professional help-seeking. A few minutes of time to support reflection, and potentially resume a peer discussion next day. Sharing of expertise and empowerment could equip this worker with knowledge, skill, confidence, and recognition of her ability and capacity to respond to the challenging set of circumstances.

A second practitioner said to her line manager, "I really messed up today...." This comment contains an element of self-reflection – if you know that you have "messed up", then it means that you have already identified the actions which you should have taken! A theoretical indirect signal of need, a worker asking for reassurance, a short discussion on what did happen versus what should have happened, and confirmation that professional development has occurred for practitioner and line manager. Listening and learning are always reciprocal.

A third worker shared her wisdom with a young student, "I have the same relationship with every family." Every human being is unique, whether parent or professional; therefore, professional–parent relationships cannot be transferred from one family to another. Each therapeutic relationship is valuable and should be personalised in response to the individual.

What does this mean in theory and practice?

Professional registration has given the early years' workforce a formal source of support mechanisms which can be used to maintain good mental and physical health, for example face to face, telephone, and online counselling services. There is also a vast network which offers informal daily support in the context of our peers. Recent research in the United Kingdom on delivery of a parenting intervention indicated that professional participants benefited from supervision sessions which incorporated opportunities for reflection, and paired working with colleagues to reduce isolation, and improve decision-making (Grayton, Burns, Pistrang, and Fearon, 2017).

In order to achieve and develop as professionals we need:

1 **To gain knowledge, understanding, and inter-personal skills.**

   Knowledge is easy to acquire from multiple sources. Understanding should be sought by the individual in relation to personal learning style and needs. Inter-personal skills can be taught within local microsystems of each organisation, under-graduate courses, or within continuous professional development opportunities. The use of positive body language, and non-judgemental phrases during professional–parent and professional–child interactions, can be promoted through role-modelling accompanied by theory. Careers are lengthy and society develops throughout generations. Every employee should observe and respond to changes in expectations, interactions, and conduct in workplaces. "Old school" is an expression which is sometimes applied to outmoded practice approaches.

2   **To recognise our achievements and reflect upon challenges.**

    Most professionals find it difficult to self-praise – self-critique is easier. Positive feedback to colleagues represents constructive teamwork; however, these interactions can be misconstrued. Peer praise can appear to have a hidden agenda, to be favour swopping, to demonstrate favouritism in teams, to divide and conquer! The theory of management needs to be put into practice with diplomacy.

3   **To respond to each other.**

    Peer support is applicable, accessible, and appropriate. Professionals will always gravitate naturally towards peers who can respond to their needs, regardless of employment hierarchy. Professional resilience can be increased formally and informally.

4   **To acknowledge that *our learning* is lifelong too.**

    It's not what you did. It's what you do next!

Conclusion

This book has presented the concept of family learning in the early years as applicable to the current generation. The future will bring further discussion concerning families, and inclusion within society. Definitions of concepts will be sought, re-configured, and influence practice in the field. Research is essential to inform policy, and to provide evidence of strengths, or to indicate areas for development in a curriculum by linking theoretical principles to practical implementation within a nursery/school, and the home environment.

Inclusive policy has resulted in an increase in the number of children attending generic services with additional support for learning needs, and it is important that care, and education are not constrained by but liberated from bureaucratic expectations. The inclusion agenda must entail discussion of these issues concerning attainment which is predicted or otherwise, at the level of politicians, professionals, parents, and the public.

72 *Leading the workforce*

Inclusive practice has enriched comprehension of educators by providing opportunities to explore the intricacies of human development, and to gain insight into the complexities of learning within a context of service provision. Concurrent influences from family and services can be merged to create an effective inclusive pedagogy which optimises learning for every child. It is an exciting time to explore theory, practice, and partnerships in a context of family learning.

It may be that statistics need to reflect and respect differences – after all inclusion is based upon a principle of celebrating diversity in mankind.

Research, policy, and practice should be used for mutual reciprocal benefit by promoting a contribution to knowledge *and* understanding, consistent application throughout a nation, and realise possibilities by evidencing human potential which transcends any preconceived outcomes.

Key messages

- Theory is the richest source of understanding for optimum practice.
- Practice illustrates and activates theory as a source of learning.
- Family learning is a multi-faceted concept which is facilitated within the early years' sector through partnership-working between professionals, parents, and extended families.
- The early years' curriculum can be underpinned through implementation beyond the organisational environment: for example, within the family home.
- Knowledge and understanding of inclusion require consideration of issues from strategic and operational levels, in addition to the needs, wants, and interests of each child.
- Inclusive pedagogy is enhanced by embracing family members as co-constructors in a child's educational journey.

References

Bergen, D., and Woodin, M. (2017). *Brain research and childhood education, implications for educators, parents and society*. Abingdon: Routledge.

Grayton, L., Burns, P., Pistrang, N., and Fearon, P. (2017). *Minding the baby, qualitative findings on implementation from the first UK service*. London: NSPCC.

Henry, J. (2001). *Creativity and perception in management*. London: Sage Publications.

Hobbs, V. (2009). Maximising the progress of learners with profound and multiple learning difficulties. *Journal of SLD Experience, volume 55, number 11*, 10–16. Retrieved May 2012, from www.bild.org.uk/our.services/journals/sld.experience/

Magnusson, D., and Stattin, H. (2006). The person in context: A holistic-interactionist approach. In W. Damon and R. Lerner (Eds.), *Handbook of child psychology* (volume 1, pp. 400–410, 418–424, 433). Hoboken, NJ: John Wiley & Sons.

Rees, K., Tully, S., and Ferguson, K. (2017). 'This is theirs': The implementation of the South Lanarkshire framework for supporting pupils with severe and profound needs. *Scottish Educational Review, volume 49, number 1*. Edinburgh: Scottish Educational Review.

Robinson, C., and Brown, A. M. (2016). Considering sensory processing issues in trauma affected children: The physical environment in children's residential homes. *Scottish Journal of Residential Child Care, volume 16, number 1*. Retrieved 10 September 2017, from www.celcis.org/knowledge.bank/search.bank/journal/Scottish-journal-residential-child-care-vol-16

Schrader-McMillan, A., and Barlow, J. (2017). *Improving the effectiveness of the child protection system – A review of literature*. Oxford: University of Oxford.

Scottish Executive. (2004). *A curriculum for excellence*. Edinburgh: Scottish Executive.

Scottish Government. (2017). *Mental health strategy*. Edinburgh: Scottish Government.

Index

Abajobir, A. A. 38
accessible source of knowledge 44–45
acquired resilience 41–43
active family learning 12–13
actualisation of genetic influences 35
actualisation of potential 20, 21–22
additional support for learning needs 32
areas for development 69
Astramovich, R. L. 55
attainment 35; inclusion and 61–64
autobiographical self 17, 44

Baby Box project 12–13
barriers to learning 38–40
Bath, H. 45
behaviour, children's 55–58
Bergen, D. 62
Bidell, T. R. 17
Blackard, S. R. 54
Blood, E. 17
Bowlby, J. 1, 4
Boxall Profile 2
Bratton, S. C. 54
Braun, D. 15
Bronfenbrenner, Urie 11–12, 35
Brown, A. M. 68
butterfly effect 51–52

Carer and Toddler Groups 8
Child-Parent-Relationship Training 54
Children and Families Act (2014) 32
Cicchetti, D. 22
Common Assessment Framework – Every Child Matters 38

Common Assessment Framework for Children and Young People 5
complementary learning 12
consistent implementation 33–34
constructive criticism 68–71
continuous professional development (CPD) 29–31
cooperative play 52
council of Scottish local authorities (COSLA) 3
culturally adapted approach 6
culturally specific approach 6
cultural sensitivity 5–6
culture of family and community learning 3
Curriculum for Excellence 37

Dance of Reciprocity 37
Davis, H. 15
deep-level learning 19–22, 50
developmental gaps 18–19

early intervention for families 33–34
Early Years Foundation Stage 4, 37
Early Years' Framework 7
Ecological Systems of Human Development 44
e-communication 10–11
Education (Scotland) Act 2016 32
Education Act (1996) 32
Effective Provision of Pre-School Education Project, The 4
Egeland, B. 17
elevated developmental functioning 38

emotional literacy 45–47
empathy 24
Enlow, M. B. 17
equity in society 7
evaluation of family learning 7–8
every child matters context 5
executive functioning 20, 21–22, 33
exosystem 12
extrapolative learning 20

Facebook 9
facilitating active family learning 13–15
family/families: and community learning, culture of 3; concept of 1; early intervention for 33–34 family learning 71–72; deep-level learning 19–22; developmental gaps and 18–19; evaluation of 7–8; facilitating active 13–15; formal 1–8; implementation of 5–6; inclusion and (see inclusion); informal 8–12; perceptions of 6–7; stages of self and 17–19; supporting active 12–13; values in 23–25; voluntary sector and 15–17
Family Partnership Model 15
financial autonomy of organisations 66
Fischer, K. W. 17
focus of attention 35
formal family learning 1–8

gaining knowledge, understanding, and inter-personal skills 70–71
gaps, developmental 18–19
genetic influences 35
Ghate, D. 33
Goodall, J. 5
good enough practice 69
good practice 66

Harris, A. 5
Heckman, J. L. 8
heritability system 35
hindsight 31

implementation of family learning 5–6; consistent 33–34
inclusion: accessible source of knowledge and 44–45; attainment and 61–64; children's behaviour and 55–58; early intervention for families and 33–34; emotional literacy and 45–47; executive function and 33; legislation 32–33; Leuven Involvement and Wellbeing Scale and 52–55; nurturing resilience in 43–50; optimum outcome 35–37; professional development and 29–31; readiness to learn and 44; reflection and 31; resilience and 38–43; responsive attachment figures and 43; self-regulation and 47–50; sensitive periods for learning and 31–32; theory to practice 34–38; in the world of learning 50–55
informal family learning 8–12
inner working model 4
in-service training 29–30
instinctive resilience 40–41
intellectual curiosity 65
intentional mental agent 17, 44, 65
intermittent interactions 52

joint effect of influences 35
Joseph, S. 4

Kellam, T. 54
knowledge: accessible source of 44–45; three different sources of 20; understanding and 30–31

Laevers, F. 19, 52
Landreth, G. L. 54
learning: barriers to 38–40; deep-level 19–22, 50; inclusion in world of 50–55; lifelong 71; readiness for 44; sensitive periods for 31–32
learning, family 71–72; deep-level learning 19–22; developmental gaps and 18–19; evaluation of 7–8; facilitating active 13–15; formal 1–8; implementation of 5–6; informal 8–12; perceptions of 6–7; stages of self and 17–19; supporting active 12–13; values in 23–25; voluntary sector and 15–17
Lee, P. 7
legislation 32–33; on formal family learning 1–8

Leuven Involvement and Wellbeing Scale 52–55
lifelong learning 71
literacy, emotional 45–47

macrosystem 12
Mansfield, P. 15
Mazzucchelli, T. G. 34
memory-initiated learning 20
mesosystem 11
microsystem 11
Miell, D. 18
mind, theory of 22
Moran, P. 33

National Occupational Standards 23
National Parenting Strategy 6
National Practice Models Getting It Right for Every Child 38
non-judgmental responses 24
nurturing resilience 43–50

optimum outcome 35–37
organisational memory 64–68

parallel play 52
Parent and Toddler Groups 8
parenting experts 5
parent's perspective 24
pedagogy 64–68
peer support 71
perceptions of family learning 6–7
personal characteristics 35
personnel 65
physical agent 17, 44
plasticity of the human brain 36
Play at Home 13
play therapy 54
poor practice 69
Positive Parenting Programme 33–34
positive regard 24
practice 64–68
professional bodies 2
professional development 29–31; gaining knowledge, understanding, and inter-personal skills in 70–71; lifelong learning and 71; peer support 71; recognising achievements and reflecting upon challenges 71

professional-parent relationship 3–5
proximal processes 35
psychological contact 23
purposeful operation 33

readiness to learn 44
reciprocal exchanges in context of learning and development 69
recognition of achievements and reflection upon challenges 71
Rees, K. 62
reflection 31
resilience 24, 38–43; acquired 41–43; barriers to learning and 38–40; instinctive 40–41; nurturing 43–50
respect 24
responsive attachment figures 43
Robinson, C. 68
Rogers, C. 23
role-modelling 4

Salamanca Statement and Framework for Action 32
Sanders, M. 33, 34
Scottish Practice Model 34
self: autobiographical 17, 44; stages of 17–19
self-recognition 18
self-regulation 47–50, 55
sensitive periods for learning 31–32
sensory level learning 19–20, 20–21
Social-Address Model 24, 65
social agent 17, 44
social media 9–11
Solihull Approach 33–34
solitary play 52
sources of knowledge, three different 20
special educational needs 32
Special Educational Needs and Disability Act (2001) 32
stages of self 17–19

teleological agent 17, 44
theory of mind 22
therapeutic alliance 3–5, 23–24
Toth, S. L. 22
transitions: children's behaviour and 56–58; workforce 66–68

translation 6
trauma, short or long-term 51–52
Triple P programme 34

United Kingdom Nurture Network 2

values, family learning 23–25
van der Kolk, B. 43
van der Merwe, A. 33
variance 35
voluntary sector 15–17
vulnerability in parents 23–24

Woodin, M. 62
workforce leadership: constructive criticism/learning and development 68–71; on inclusion and attainment 61–64; organisational memory, pedagogy, and practice in 64–68; practice to policy 61; during transition periods 66–68
Wright, R. J. 17
Wright, R. O. 17